WORKING POINTERS AND SETTERS

WORKING POINTERS AND SETTERS

DAVID HUDSON

SWAN·HILL
PRESS

Copyright © 2004 David Hudson

First published in the UK in 2004
by Swan Hill Press, an imprint of Quiller Publishing Ltd

British Library Cataloguing-in-Publication Data
   A catalogue record for this book
   is available form the British Library

ISBN 0 904057 40 3

Printed in China

Swan Hill Press
An imprint of Quiller Publishing Ltd.
Wykey House, Wykey, Shrewsbury, SY4 1JA
Tel: 01939 261616 Fax: 01939 261606
E-mail: info@quillerbooks.com
Website: www.swanhillbooks.com

CONTENTS

CHAPTER 1
Introduction

But if a brace of grouse you'd kill,
On twenty-three square miles of hill,
My best advice is, go and get a
Pointer, or an Irish Setter,
Don walking boots, take up your gun,
Then turn him loose and watch him run.

David Hudson

In the modern world of driven shoots and breech-loading shotguns, pointers and setters are something of an anachronism: a living, and sometimes working, reminder of past times when shooting was a more leisurely and less commercial pursuit. Our native game birds, the grey partridge on agricultural land and the red grouse on the moor, were the main sporting quarries in those days and they were shot over pointing dogs. The time of the big battue, the reared pheasant and the commercial shoot were yet to come, though the dual pressures of technological innovation and Victorian fashion would eventually bring about a decline in popularity of the pointing breeds as working dogs.

The essence of pointer and setter work is to find game.

The essence of pointer and setter work is to find game. Their quarry, in Britain, may be partridge or grouse, pheasant, ptarmigan, blackgame, snipe or woodcock: while overseas birddogs are worked on quail, willow grouse, sand grouse, guinea fowl, sage hen, francolin and any other game bird that will sit to a dog – that is to say, will attempt to avoid a potential predator by concealment rather than by taking to the wing at the first intimation of danger. It is this fortunate combination of a quarry that will sit tightly in front of a dog that will remain on point that makes birddog work possible.

Pointing dogs are at their best – which is to say at their most useful – when their quarry is thin on the ground. If you have twenty beaters working through a wood containing several hundred pheasants there is no need for a pointer or setter to find birds for you. If dogs are needed at all then spaniels, Labradors or even terriers will do the job far better. But if your desire is to shoot grouse on the open hill, where there may be scores – even hundreds – of acres of empty heather between each covey, then there is nothing to compare with a pointer or a setter to find those birds for you, and then to afford you the best possible chance of getting a shot at them. If you are a falconer, needing time to release your peregrine and allow it to gain height before producing game for it to stoop on, then a pointing dog is vital to your sport. And if you enjoy hunting for game rather than sitting on a shooting stick while a team of beaters does all the hard work for you, then shooting over pointing dogs may be just the sport for you.

8   *Pointing dogs are a vital part of the falconer's team.*

The modern gamekeeper, rearing and releasing pheasants and partridges, can manage his birds by the strategic siting of release pens and feed rides so that he knows exactly where to find them on a shoot day. Wild game, by its very nature, lives where it chooses, and provides the sportsman with an entirely different challenge. The game will not come to him; therefore he must get out and find the birds. Pointers and setters were developed to fulfil this particular requirement.

The nature and habits of wild game dictated the physical makeup of the dogs that were bred to hunt it. If the quarry was to be found hidden in thick cover then a dog that would drive into the cover and force it out was required. A tough, sturdy body and a thick coat, allied to the courage and determination to face such cover combined to give us the ancestors of our modern spaniels. Wildfowlers needed dogs that were happy to swim in freezing water to retrieve ducks and geese and developed strong, water-loving dogs with heavy coats, soft mouths and highly developed retrieving instincts. Coursing hares demands speed, strength, agility and excellent eyesight – precisely the characteristics of a working greyhound. It is the nature of the game that determines the nature of the dog.

Partridge and grouse, living on arable land and moorland respectively, present a different problem for the sportsman. Both attempt to evade their enemies by hiding in stubble, roots or heather and crouching invisibly until danger has passed. When they feel discovery is inevitable they seek refuge in sudden, swift flight. The need to find such birds but not to flush them until the gun, the falcon or, in the past, the netsman, was in position is the reason that today's setters and pointers exist in their familiar forms.

A dog that is going to hunt over wide acreages needs stamina, speed and the determination to carry on working even when game is scarce. These requirements lay out the physical make-up of the birddog. He must have pace and power without carrying excess weight: his legs must be long enough to cope with heather, stubble and roots, but strong enough to stand the stresses and strains that steep slopes and broken ground will impose on them. His coat must not be so heavy that he will toil in the heat of August, nor so light that he will suffer from wet and cold later in the season. He must have the speed to take in a good rake of ground combined with the stamina to keep running at speed for more than just a brief sprint. The correct balance between pace and endurance is one that engenders lively argument among pointer and setter enthusiasts, and something that we will be returning to in later chapters.

Physically, pointers and setters do not run to extremes. Greyhounds are the sprinters of the dog world: capable of blistering speed, but only able to sustain it for a few moments. Sled dogs, at the opposite end of the spectrum, perhaps best represent the marathon runners, maintaining a steady pace for hour after hour without seeming to require any rest. Pointers and setters lie neatly between these two extremes.

Pace is essential if a dog is to cover enough ground to enable a shooting party to make sensible progress across field or moor. A slow, but wide-ranging dog would condemn a shooting party to shuffling forward a few yards at a time with long pauses between each movement. On the other hand, if your dogs only had pace without deep reserves of stamina a shooting day would be impossible unless a whole kennel full was on hand to share the work. Putting these features together brings us to the typical setter or pointer: a medium sized dog carrying no excess weight, nicely proportioned, long on the leg, though not excessively so, light of coat, long tailed for balance and bursting with energy and enthusiasm for his work.

If we are to invoke a human analogy, the pointer or setter best compares to a middle distance runner, with power and pace combined in a spare but well muscled frame. It is a combination that has resulted in dogs that are particularly pleasing to the eye with their symmetry, balance, graceful movement and elegant build. Add the rich, copper coat of the Irish

Power and pace combined in a spare, but well-muscled, frame.

Setter or the black and tan of the Gordon: the varied colours and handsome head of the English Setter or the stark contrasts of black and white or liver and white of the Pointer and it is immediately apparent why these dogs are today in such demand in the show ring and as pets in addition to their role in the sporting field.

In one respect pointers and setters do run to an extreme. I am referring to their powers of scenting. All gundogs rely on their noses more than their eyes when it comes to finding and retrieving game, but none of the breeds have had developed their sense of smell to the extent that it has been refined in pointers and setters. Again, this is down to the nature of the game: birddogs have to find game out in the open without flushing it, and this means they must locate their quarry at a sufficient distance to positively identify it before they close in to the point at which the birds decide that flight is a better alternative than concealment. And since they will be finding the quarry using scent alone – not sight, not sound, but scent only – it follows that one of the prime characteristics that the first breeders of birddogs will have selected for was scenting ability.

It is clear that those early breeders, as they refined their bloodlines to produce the familiar breeds of today, were concerned with aesthetic qualities as well as working ability. A great deal of the pleasure of a day on the hill, shooting over pointing dogs, comes from watching the dogs at work. There are many parallels in the hunting world where much of the joy of a day in the field comes from watching hounds: not from the final act of killing fox, hare or deer. It is the dog work that delights.

The sight of a pointer or setter racing effortlessly across a hill face with that elegance of movement that so characterises the breeds is enough to lift the spirits of the dourest of sportsmen. At rest they are equally pleasing with soft eyes, well-proportioned heads, happy expressions and lean, lithe bodies. My own love affair with Irish Setters began over thirty years ago when a handsome red dog trotted, uninvited into my office and grinned at me across my desk. I was so struck with his friendly nature, good looks and general air of bonhomie that I determined then and there to enhance my newly married household with one just like him.

I might have reflected at the time on just why he was wandering the streets of Eye without supervision. I have, of course, since learned that wandering off to explore, to hunt or simply to make new friends is something of a feature of Irish Setters. Certainly, in the years since then I have lost count of the hours I have spent and the miles I must have walked in search of setters or pointers that have slipped away from home, or while out on the hill, in order to spend a little time following their own agenda.

I have referred to the pointing breeds as something of an anachronism in the modern shooting world. Where once shooting over pointers or setters was the norm for the country sportsman it is now very much the exception. Grouse still live on the moors of course, though the area of moorland available to them has much declined, but the wild grey partridge has become something of a rare bird in the last few decades.

The causes of the decline in wild game over the past fifty odd years have been the subject of much debate, many experiments and a great deal of scientific research. The intensification of agriculture and the resultant specialisation of cropping, the loss of habitat as hedgerows were grubbed out, moorland turned to grazing and wetlands drained, the almost universal application

Working out a point on grouse. Time spent on the hill with a pointer or setter is never time wasted.

11

of herbicides and insecticides to crops and the replacement of men with machines have all contributed, along with a drastic reduction in the number of professional gamekeepers.

Although wild game has decreased dramatically, reared partridges and, particularly, pheasants have more than replaced it. In addition social change has meant that shooting has become accessible to a much wider range of people, and improvements in roads and transport have brought it within their reach. Instead of 'the squire and his relations' having exclusive access to the shooting rights in their parish it is far more likely today that shoots will be run by a syndicate of guns from all walks of life. Instead of one or two friends setting out to harvest the naturally occurring wild game, the modern shoot will entail a team of beaters working together to send a stream of reared birds over a line of standing guns. There will be work for spaniels as flushing dogs and for Labradors, Flatcoats and Goldens as retrievers, but sadly, there is little demand on a driven shoot for the pointer or the setter.

I do not write this as a criticism or a condemnation of the way shooting is run today. Indeed, I am actively involved in the keepering and management of just such a syndicate shoot and thoroughly enjoy both the sport it gives me and the challenges that it presents. I am doubly fortunate in that I can also devote a good deal of my time to my pointers and setters: to training, working and just enjoying their company. However much I enjoy driven shooting, beating or picking-up with my Labrador, it is out on the hill that I am happiest: working a pointer or a setter, watching them flow across the ground with that elegant, effortless movement and then crash on to point at the first scent of a covey.

It doesn't matter whether I am carrying a gun myself, working the dogs so that others may have the pleasure of shooting over them, carrying out a grouse count for one of my keeper friends, or simply putting in some time on a training session. Time spent on the hill is never wasted, and time spent on the hill in company with a pointer or setter is quality time indeed. (I will say nothing at this juncture about time spent on the hill looking for a pointer or setter that has vanished over the horizon and failed to return.)

My aim in this book is to try to convey to the reader some of the pleasure – yes, and some of the frustration – that comes from owning, training and working pointers and setters. Since the great majority of pointers and setters are kept as pets rather than as working dogs I will not concentrate exclusively on their working role but consider them as companions and show dogs as well as workers in the shooting field or at field trials. If, as may happen, some of you are persuaded to try and make the transition from pet owner to working owner then I hope that the book will help you in that aim. I can guarantee that your pointer or setter will approve of the change.

In general in this book I refer to pointers and setters using male pronouns – 'he' and 'him' rather than 'she' or 'her'. This represents no bias on my part: simply a determination not to clutter the book with constant reference to 'he or she' and 'his or hers', which I feel is both awkward and unnecessary. Throughout the book you may assume that 'he' also means 'she', except where it obviously does not, as in matters of breeding for example.

CHAPTER 2
History

*Domesticated Dogs Finding Their Game By Scent, But Not Killing
It, Being
Chiefly Used In Aid Of The Gun.
The Dog In Health & Disease* – Longmans, Green & Co 1859

Such is the heading of the chapter covering pointers and setters in Stonehenge's comprehensive work on dogs published around a hundred and fifty years ago. The term 'Gun Dogs' would pretty well cover all the dogs described in the chapter, with the exception of the Dalmatian, though Stonehenge remarks that 'Though this peculiarly marked variety of the species is only used in Great Britain as a carriage dog, in his native country he is made to stand very steadily at game, and is employed in aid of the gun exactly as are our "Pontos" and "Dons"'. The Poodle is also included in this chapter, though the Labrador is not, appearing in the later chapter on 'Pastoral Dogs and Those Used for Draught'.

Several of the varieties of gun dog described by Stonehenge are no longer found in Britain or have been absorbed into one of the other species. The Russian Setter, the Welsh Setter, Northern Irish Water Spaniel, Southern Irish Water Spaniel and English Water Spaniel, the Spanish Pointer and the Portuguese Pointer have all disappeared in the past hundred and fifty years, and the illustrations of some of the breeds that are still with us show considerable differences to the appearance of those same breeds today. If so much change can take place over such a short time, then think how much the dog has altered since man first started meddling with nature in order to change the basic canine to meet his own requirements.

It is generally accepted that the domestic dog of today is a descendant of the wolf, though not necessarily a direct descendant of the wolves that still exist today. It is considered by some authorities that today's dogs may have their roots in a now extinct branch of the wolf family. Certainly dogs, wolves, jackals, bears and the like have common ancestors among the Canids of the Pleistocene period. Back in pre-historic times early man must have started his relationship with the dog by taking wolf cubs from their den, then presumably progressed to breeding his own wolves instead of capturing them from the wild. The subsequent development of the dog from semi-wild wolf living alongside man in his cave to the myriad of breeds we know today will have happened gradually over many thousands of years but is, of course, not documented until the last few hundred, by which time the bulk of that development had already taken place.

It is reasonable to suppose that wolves themselves will have changed both physically and behaviourally during the period in which the domestic dog was evolving. The wolves we can see today represent only a snapshot from history, the legacy of many thousands of years of natural selection. Artificial selection as practised in breeding programmes devised by man can bring about physical and behavioural changes in an animal in a much shorter time than will happen in the wild, but even so, wild animals are still evolving as the principal of 'survival of the fittest' gradually eliminates those least well equipped to survive.

It is not difficult to 'see' the wolf in many of our modern breeds such as German Shepherds and Huskies, though the wolfish characteristics of a Chihuahua or a Shih Tzu are somewhat less obvious to the eye. Even so, though physically most of the dogs of today bear little resemblance to their lupine ancestors, many of the instincts of those wolves are still there to be seen. Consider the natural history of the wolf in comparison with the domestic dog.

Most species of wolves live and hunt in packs. Within their pack they are hierarchical, territorial and cooperative in hunting and rearing young. They hunt by sight and scent, variously chasing, herding and ambushing their prey; they carry food to their young and defend their territory from other wolves. These are the basic instincts that have been developed in the dog to produce the guarding, herding and hunting breeds of today.

Today there are sheep and cattle dogs used to gather, drive and herd our flocks of domestic animals using the same methods that wolves use when hunting caribou. Wolves drive prey animals so that the weaker specimens fall back and become easy prey in exactly the same way that a Border Collie will harry and hustle a flock of sheep into moving to where the shepherd requires them. When that collie swoops in to isolate a single animal from the flock it is behaving exactly as its wild cousins do when they cut out a young or a sickly beast from the relative safety of the herd.

Guard dogs defending a factory site or pet dogs threatening intruders to 'their' garden are obeying the same territorial instincts that a pack of wolves follows in protecting their hunting territory from neighbouring packs. A Labrador proudly bearing a shot pheasant back to its owner is following the same instinct that drives a wolf to carry prey back to the den for its mate and cubs: a Cocker Spaniel diving headlong into a bramble patch to evict a cock pheasant is acting in exactly the same way as a wolf pouncing on its prey. These similarities are clear and unequivocal.

Now let us consider a pointer or setter, winding a covey of grouse and instantly freezing, motionless, twenty yards from them.

At first sight, standing still twenty or thirty yards from your prey, and staying there until someone comes along and tells you to close in and flush it, may not have obvious survival advantages. In fact, quite the opposite would seem to be the case, as any hunting animal that

14   *A Pointer scenting a covey of grouse and freezing motionless a few yards from them.*

automatically ceased to hunt when still out of range of its intended prey would seem destined for swift consignment to the great dustbin of evolution along with the dinosaur, the Dodo and the Passenger Pigeon. In order to understand the pointing instinct we need to look closer at the way in which some predators hunt, or more specifically, the way in which they bring a hunt to a successful conclusion. First though we should consider the way in which selective breeding has exaggerated certain characteristics of wolfish behaviour and subdued others in order to produce the specialised skills of certain of our present day domestic dogs.

For centuries man has kept dogs to perform specific tasks such as guarding, herding and hunting. It is natural that when breeding from these dogs that man chooses as parent stock those individuals that are best at their particular task. If you want a guard dog that will protect your person and your property your major requirements are likely to be size and aggression. A hunting dog, depending on the type of game you are intending to hunt, may be selected for its pace in running down fleet-footed animals, for its ability to find and flush small game from cover or for its courage when facing dangerous animals such as boar or bear. If you want a dog to drag a sledge or a travois then you will be looking for strength and endurance. This is selective breeding for a particular characteristic and, over time, will have the effect of making that characteristic more and more pronounced.

In nature, the right to mate with female members of the pack is controlled by less specific methods of selection. To survive in the wild requires a mix of skills rather than a super-abundance of any particular skill, and wolf-pack hierarchy has evolved around this. There is no advantage to being the fastest wolf in the pack if pace is attained at the expense of stamina: no advantage in being the biggest if size brings a loss of pace and agility along with a need for ever greater amounts of food that you are no longer fast enough to catch. As a result, natural selection tends to be a pretty slow process, and wild animals, having once found a successful formula for survival, tend to breed to the average rather than to the extreme.

But man comes along and starts to meddle with the natural order of things. He takes the biggest and most aggressive of his tamed wolves and he breeds from them to produce even bigger and more aggressive offspring. He takes the fastest runners and mates them together in order to produce hunting dogs with the speed to course a hare or a deer. Breeding and selecting for a particular characteristic for generation after generation will enhance that characteristic far more swiftly than can occur with natural selection. Where nature produces wolves that stay pretty much the same for centuries, man produces dogs that evolve at a quite spectacular rate.

It is variously estimated that from around ten thousand years at a minimum, up to fifty thousand years or even more have passed since man first began his relationship with dogs. If we could journey back to the time when the first wolf joined forces with man it is likely that the wolves then existing would be recognisable as, and perhaps almost identical to, the wolves that we know today. It is quite certain that there would be nothing existing that resembled most of today's domestic dogs. And yet, from those first tamed wolves all of today's variations on the theme of dog have since descended, while the wolf has remained basically the same.

But what about our ancestral birddog that we left a few paragraphs back, standing staunchly on point? How, and why did man selectively breed dogs for their ability to point game? And where does that ability arise?

In the wild predators typically find their prey by using one or more of their senses of sight, scent and hearing. The use of the sight is a very direct way of hunting: if you can see your prey then you know exactly where it is and what you have to do in order to catch it. Scent and sound though are less specific. Imagine yourself standing in a wood. It is quiet all around you and then, suddenly, you hear a noise – a gentle rustling as a squirrel scratches among the fallen leaves. You want to see that squirrel, so what do you do? You stand quite still and listen intently

Hundreds of years of selective breeding refined and enhanced the natural pointing instinct in birddogs.

as you try and pinpoint the source of the sound, turning your head to face the direction from which the rustling appears to be coming. If you watch a cat hunting a hedgerow for mice and voles you will see it doing exactly the same thing: pricking its ears at the first tiny rustle and then freezing as it tries to pin the sound down to its exact source.

An animal hunting its prey by scent does much the same. It catches the first whiff of the prey on the breeze and flares its nostrils to confirm and locate the source of the scent, just as the cat pricks up its ears to catch more of the sound. If it is on the move when it hits the scent it slows or stops: the prey is somewhere nearby and the next thing is to decide exactly where it is. It is this first reaction: stopping and checking the first sound or scent of prey: that is the origin of the point. The length of time that a wild animal will spend 'on point' is usually just sufficient for it to move on to the next stage in the hunting process.

This initial 'freezing' of motion in a wild animal is usually the prelude to moving in on the prey and either pouncing on it or flushing it from cover so that it can be chased down. In the wild the objective of the hunt is always for the hunter to end up with paws, claws or teeth on and in the prey. In the case of a hunting cat for example there may be a prolonged period 'on point' as it waits for the mouse to make another move – and thus another sound – before it is certain enough of its position to pounce. A dog – pointing by scent rather than sound – does much the same thing as it uses its powers of scent to narrow down the location of its prey, and it is this natural instinct to stop and check the source of a scent that has been greatly refined over the centuries to produce the classic pointing breeds of today.

A wild dog that concluded a hunt by pointing its prey and never moved on to the pounce and kill stage would have a pretty short stay on the evolutionary ladder. The same would have been true of man's early hunting dogs. Their job would have been to catch and kill: not to simply warn of the presence of game. It is only in relatively recent times, when hunting has become a sport rather than a means of survival, that man would have any use for a pointing

dog. Those early hunting dogs would presumably have been used by their masters to hunt in much the same way as a wild wolf hunted, that is, they would have run down prey that was too swift for man to catch himself. Only as man developed more refined methods of hunting would the dog have been developed to aid him in making the kill rather than killing the prey themselves.

Falconry and netting are two hunting methods in which a dog that points its prey rather than flushing it gives the hunter an advantage. The two differ substantially in that falconry was a sport, for gentlemen, whereas netting was a way of killing game for the larder. In falconry the pointer is used to make the killing of game more exciting: in netting to make it more efficient. In both cases though, a pointing dog is essential.

There are few more exciting sights in field sports than that of a peregrine stooping from two or three hundred feet in the sky to kill a fleeing grouse or partridge. It is in order to allow the falcon to gain height in anticipation of the stoop that the pointing dog is used. The falcon is carried, hooded, on the falconer's wrist.

Peregrine falcons were used to kill game over pointing dogs long before the development of the gun as a sporting weapon.

17

When the dog points to indicate the presence of game the bird is cast off and spirals up into the sky high above the pointing dog. Then, when the falconer is satisfied that his falcon has reached a sufficient height, he orders the pointing dog in to flush its quarry, and the flight is under way.

It is the use of a pointing dog that gives the falconer control over his sport. If he uses a flushing dog such as a spaniel he will have to have his falcon aloft and waiting on from the moment the dog starts hunting. There is then the danger that the falcon may become bored and take off on business of its own if game is not found quickly, or stoop on small birds that are flushed as the dog hunts. Alternatively, he can launch the bird from his fist when the quarry is first flushed, but this just results in a stern chase that lacks the excitement and spectacle of the stoop from on high. When worked in conjunction with an experienced pointing dog though the falcon and dog strike up a partnership. The bird knows that the point is the prelude to a stoop, and with the dog motionless and locked onto the scent of the game there is far less danger of a wasted stoop on a blackbird or pipit.

Netting game was not so much a sport as a way of filling the larder. When a dog pointed the handlers would draw a net right over the dog and – hopefully – the game that it was pointing. Setters are generally reckoned to have been developed with this in mind, and their habit of 'setting' to game – sometimes to the extent of dropping almost flat on the ground when on point – would have been more conducive to the practice of netting than the typical, upright stance of the modern pointer. Having said that, many setters stand tall when on point, and not a few pointers will crouch low to the ground. It is always dangerous to generalise when writing about dogs.

I have never tried to net game in this manner. Indeed, I believe to do so would be against the law, unless it was done under licence, though I believe that Derry Argue, a well-known and well-respected pointer and setter man from the north of Scotland has done so, under licence, in the course of a grouse research project. In his book *Pointers and Setters* (Swan Hill, 1993) he refers to it as 'a deadly method of taking game'.

At first thought it might seem unlikely that any wild bird would sit still long enough to make it possible to draw a net over it. However, I have seen grouse sitting so tightly that one of the guns coming in to a point has actually trodden on them before they would attempt to fly. This is particularly true early in the season when the young birds are less strong on the wing and instinct tells them that they are more likely to escape a predator by clapping down motionless in the heather than by taking flight. This would certainly be true if the predator in question was a peregrine, but obviously not if it was a fox, stoat, dog, or indeed, two men with a net.

But netting has gone forever, outside of research projects, and although pointers and setters are still very much the choice of the falconer the majority of those that work in the field today are used for shooting. It was the development of the shotgun, from about the middle of the seventeenth century that made possible the sport of shooting birds on the wing. As the sport grew so did the demand for dogs that could find game for the gun and gundogs began to emerge.

The early forms of sporting guns looked superficially pretty much like the guns we use today. They certainly worked on the same principle. You take a tube that is sealed at one end and put some gunpowder into that tube, followed by some form of projectile. Point the tube at your target: set fire to the powder, and the gases created as the powder burns will expand and push the projectile out of the tube and on towards whatever you are aiming at. This may be anything from a bird to a battleship: the projectile may be half an ounce of lead shot or half a ton of shell casing packed with high explosive: but the principle remains the same. The main thing that changed over the years was the method of ignition, or the manner in which the gunner set fire to the powder charge.

The earliest guns were set off with a smouldering piece of string that was applied directly to the gunpowder through a touchhole drilled through the barrel, but the first reasonably efficient method of firing a gun was the flintlock. A piece of flint was brought into sharp contact with a steel, using some sort of spring loaded mechanism called a 'lock'. The sparks from this contact were used to set fire to a pinch of powder in a priming pan, which in turn ignited the main charge inside the barrel. As the lock mechanism was refined it became an efficient method of firing a gun and the sport of shooting game on the wing came into being.

A flintlock is considerably more exciting to fire than one of today's modern, breech-loading shotguns. When sparks from the flint ignite the powder in the pan there is a flash and a little cloud of smoke interspersed with sparks, jets out right in front of the face of the gunner. There is then a slight but perceptible delay before the main charge ignites and spews smoke, fire and shot out of the end of the barrel. The prudent user of a flintlock will wear safety glasses when firing it since there is a very real danger of sparks flying back into their eyes – not something

that troubles us today with our boxlocks and sidelocks and over and unders. In essence though, the flintlock and the breech-loader differ only in the detail of their construction. The principles employed and the methods of working are exactly the same – until it is time to reload.

Reloading a muzzle-loading weapon takes time. First the gun is stood upright with the butt on the ground and the muzzle (or muzzles) pointing to the sky. The gunner takes his powder flask and pours a measure of powder down the barrel. Then a wad is placed in the end of the barrel and the ramrod is withdrawn from its hoops beneath the barrel, reversed so that the rammer is pointing downwards and thrust down the barrel to seat the wad firmly on top of the powder charge. Next the shot flask is used to pour a measure of shot down on top of the over-powder wad, then an over-shot wad is placed in the muzzle and rammed down with the ramrod. The rod is then reversed and replaced in its hoops.

If you are dealing with a percussion gun the hammer is drawn back to half-cock and a percussion cap is set on the nipple. If the gun is a flintlock it too is set to half-cock and then the hammer is lifted to allow a pinch of powder to be placed in the pan. The hammer is then let down to cover the pan and the cock

Re-loading a muzzle-loader is a fiddly business and takes considerable time.

Clouds of smoke obscure the view after a shot at grouse with a muzzle-loader.

pulled back to full-cock. Only then are you ready to fire. (Note that the 'hammer' of a flintlock is the piece of steel that covers the pan, and is struck by the flint, gripped in the jaws of the cock, to produce the spark. With the advent of percussion locks the term 'hammer' was used to refer to the part of the mechanism formerly called the 'cock'.)

While it is said that experienced and well-drilled soldiers during the Peninsular Campaign could fire three or four rounds a minute from their muskets, particularly when spurred on by the sight and sound of a French column approaching with bayonets fixed, in the shooting field a more leisurely rate of fire was the norm. Whether walking in line or shooting over pointing dogs the system was the same. Once game was flushed and a shot had been fired proceedings were halted to allow the gun to be reloaded. It followed therefore that the guns themselves had to be in control of the rate at which game would be produced. The development of the breech-loading shotgun and the fact that a sportsman could now fire, reload and fire again within a matter of seconds brought about a revolution in the way shooting was organised: a revolution that was to have far-reaching consequences for pointers and setters.

The coming of the breech-loading shotgun opened the way for the driven shoot. With a double-barrelled breech-loader allowing both barrels to be re-loaded within the space of perhaps three or four seconds it became possible, in theory at least, for a sportsman to keep up a rate of fire of perhaps forty shots in the space of a minute. If he used two guns and employed a loader this might rise to sixty shots a minute. In practice of course it is unlikely in the extreme that even the most over-stocked of shoots would produce enough birds for this rate of fire to actually be required, but it is certainly possible for an experienced gun with a modern shotgun to fire two shots, re-load and fire two more shots within five seconds. Such speed would have been beyond all expectations of the gunner armed with a muzzle-loader.

The advent of shotguns that could be reloaded quickly soon brought about a change in the way game shooting was organised. Instead of the sportsman having to walk the fields, woods or moors to where the game was lying he could stand at a peg or in a butt and have the game driven over him. And, because it was now possible to fire lots of shots in a short time, the shoot organisers began to arrange things so that there would be enough game to allow just that to happen. There was no need to wait for half a minute or so after every shot so that the gun could be re-loaded: the partridge, grouse or pheasant could be flushed from cover and sent winging towards the guns in rapid succession. The Victorian 'battue' had arrived.

Whether the coming of driven game shooting was a great advance, or whether it represented the end of true, sporting shooting is a matter of opinion. It is a fact though, that where pointers and setters had been an essential part of the shooting scene prior to the coming of the breech-loader, they quickly became marginalised once the driven shoot arrived.

The job of a pointer or setter is firstly to show by pointing that it has found game, and then to remain on point until the gun has walked to within range of where the game is hiding. If you have several hundred pheasants collected in one corner of a covert though, there is no need for a pointing dog to tell you where they are, and if your objective is simply to flush the game towards a distant line of guns there is no advantage in a dog that points. Once found the birds can be got on the wing immediately. They are going to the guns now instead of the guns coming to them.

So as driven game shooting 'took over' from the older practice of walking up game the need for pointers and setters declined. A flushing dog like a spaniel could be used in the beating line but there was no longer a place for the sort of wide-ranging, hard running dogs that had once ruled the shooting field. The decline of the birddog was rapid, but it was never terminal. In some parts of the country such as the far north of Scotland, where areas were vast and game was thinly spread, driven shooting was never a viable proposition and the old-fashioned methods of shooting over pointers continued – and continues to the present day.

It is not difficult to see why driven game shooting rapidly became 'the rage' for the Victorian sportsman. Shooting over pointing dogs was not a sport for the armchair sportsman. Walking for hours across fields and moors, carrying a gun, powder and shot, and quite possibly the shot game puts a premium on fitness. Training and working pointers and setters takes time, patience, a certain amount of ability and requires access to suitable training ground. Shooting over dogs demands much more than just marksmanship. The ability to 'read' a dog, to get into the right position for the shot, to 'stalk' the birds when wind and weather make them wild are all vital to success. In contrast driven shooting can be enjoyed by anyone who can stagger a few yards from carriage to peg, and point a gun in the general direction of the birds that are flying over him.

This is not intended to pour scorn on driven shooting, either now or a hundred and fifty years ago. In many ways the advent of the battue opened up the sport of shooting to guns who would have been unwilling or unable to make the effort required in walking up partridges or shooting grouse over dogs. Though no doubt the change was deplored by many who saw themselves as 'true sportsmen', driven shooting became the fashion, and the need for pointing dogs declined as the demand for retrievers increased.

Although the numbers of *working* pointers and setters declined enormously with the coming of the driven shoot the breeds were, and still are, much in demand in the show ring, and as house pets. Inevitably the requirements of the show ring differ markedly from those of the sportsman and over the past century or so setters and pointers have been divided into two main

21

types: the working strains and the show/pet strains. Within these broad categories there are many sub-divisions brought about as show dogs have been bred so as to emphasise certain physical points, or working (and particularly trialling) dogs have been bred for speed, or stamina or staunchness or some other trait that was considered particularly desirable.

The modern Pointer is generally supposed to have originated from the Spanish Pointer: a dog that appears, in the few contemporary pictures of it, to have been a much heavier, and presumably slower, dog than its slim, racy descendants. There is a well known and much used woodcut of a 'Spanish Pointer' that shows a stocky, heavily muscled dog on point. From the build of the dog in this picture it is inferred that Spanish Pointers were all bulky, slow animals.

Now it is possible that such an inference is absolutely correct, but I feel a degree of caution is warranted. Paintings of farm animals from the same period typically show pigs, sheep and cattle with enormous bodies borne on short, thin legs. Pictures of horses galloping regularly depict the animals with their legs extended fore and aft in the manner of an elongated rocking horse – a gait that a horse simply does not employ in real life. Do we infer from such contemporary paintings that farm animals were once shaped like OXO cubes, or that horses galloped with an entirely different gait? Of course we do not. Why then do some observers read quite so much into a picture of a dog produced in the same period?

The setters share common ancestry with spaniels: indeed they were referred to as 'setting spaniels' right up to the beginning of the eighteenth century. It is not difficult to see the link between the breeds even today, nor to visualise the manner in which the setting spaniels became split into the two families of setters and the spaniels that we know today. By definition a dog that points or setts is a dog that can be worked over a wider range than a dog that flushes game as soon as it finds it. And a dog that is expected to range widely needs long legs to carry it over the ground with the minimum of effort. The two characteristics that most obviously distinguish setters from spaniels are their instinct to point game and their longer legs.

There is a third and arguably equally vital requirement for a pointing dog, and that is the need for the dog to have a 'long' nose. This does not mean long in the physical sense, but in the sense of the distance from which the dog is capable of detecting game. My Labrador will point pheasants when she is working in the beating line, but invariably the bird she is pointing will be within a yard or so of her nose. In order to point game consistently without flushing it a pointing dog has to detect sufficient scent to induce a point at such a distance that the birds consider that concealment rather than flight is their best defensive strategy. Late in the season, when grouse are becoming wild, this could be anything up to forty or fifty yards. There are certainly dogs that can find birds at such distances, though there are not many guns with sufficient field craft to manoeuvre themselves into range for a shot.

Selecting and breeding from those dogs that were best suited for the respective tasks of flushing or pointing game would have gone a long way towards producing both the spaniels and the setters that exist today. In addition to breeding for those essential characteristics though, breeders also choose bloodlines that they hope will produce offspring with other features that are considered desirable. The overall size of the dog, the length, thickness and colour of its coat, the temperament, the colour of the eyes even can all be major influences in a breeding programme.

Over the centuries the blood-lines of the various pointing breeds have been mixed and mingled both within the 'family' of pointing dogs and by having out-crosses introduced in order to influence and (in theory) improve traits such as stamina, pace, nose and coat. Crosses with foxhounds have been well documented as breeders looked for extra stamina from their gundogs, and the influence of the greyhound is evident in certain early photographs of pointers. Oddities such as rough-coated pointers, white Gordon Setters and red and white Irish Setters (of

Gordon Setters were bred to cope with the harsh climate of the Scottish Highlands.

This black Pointer clearly shows the influence of the greyhound crosses used by eighteenth century breeders to inject pace into their dogs.

23

which much more later) all show characteristics that are a throwback to earlier days when the gene pools available to breeders were not conscribed by the iron hand of the Kennel Club.

It is only in relatively recent times that breeders have been induced to believe that only 'pure' bloodlines were acceptable. Our modern gundogs are the result of hundreds of years of selection and experimentation by breeders who sought to improve the appearance, the working ability and the temperament of their animals. That we have largely closed our eyes to the possibilities of further improving our pointers and setters by selective crossing is perhaps a symptom of the arrogance of modern man. It took our ancestors thousands of years to develop the basic dog into the myriad of varieties that are recognised across the world as 'pure-bred'. To assume that no further improvements can be made in the future is more than a little presumptuous.

But having said that, it is hard to imagine a more perfect sight than a pointer at full gallop across a heather covered hill under a hot August sun. Few dogs in the show ring can match the grace, elegance and flowing movement of an Irish Setter. And since the great majority of pointers and setters neither work for the gun nor compete in the show ring we must also recognise the fact that for many – probably the majority of – pointer and setter owners all that matters is that these handsome dogs can make loving and loyal pets.

The sportsmen who invested so much time and effort into developing the ancestors of our modern Pointers, Irish Setters, English Setters and Gordon Setters may not have had either the show ring or the hearthrug in mind when they were planning their breeding strategy, but on both counts they seem to have done a pretty good job albeit unintentionally.

Shooting over pointers and setters demands a degree of fitness from guns and handler as well as from the dogs.

CHAPTER 3
The Breeds

There is another sort of land Spannyels which are called Setters.
The Country Farme Surflet and Markham 1616

There are, at the time of writing four so-called 'British' breeds of pointing dog. Or perhaps there are five, or maybe six. And just to complicate the matter further, it is generally believed that all four 'British' breeds were developed from dogs that originated on the continent – the Spanish Pointer being the ancestor of the Pointer and the various setter varieties being descended from spaniels, which themselves supposedly got their generic name because they originated in Spain.

In addition to our 'native' pointing breeds a dozen or so 'continental' pointers have established residence here over the past sixty years or so and there is no doubt that others will arrive. The German Shorthaired Pointer, German Wirehaired Pointer, Weimaraner, Hungarian Vizsla, Hungarian Wirehaired Vizsla, Brittany Spaniel, Large Munsterlander, Italian Spinone, Wirehaired Pointing Griffon and the Bracco Italiano are all here now in greater or lesser numbers, some having been here well over half a century while others are relative newcomers. I wonder if someone writing a book on 'Pointers and Setters' a couple of hundred years from now will be discussing ten or fifteen 'British' breeds of pointing dog on account of some or all of these 'outsiders' having by then been fully accepted and integrated into our list of 'native' breeds?

Pointers and setters are not normally asked to retrieve but many will do so if allowed.

But for the moment I am only proposing to consider the four (or five, or six) pointing breeds that are generally considered as 'British' at the time of writing. Of these the Pointer, English Setter, Irish Setter (or Red Setter) and Gordon Setter are the four universally accepted breeds. In addition the Red and White Irish Setter has been re-established in Britain since around 1980, making a fifth 'British' pointing breed, and there are a number of English Setter enthusiasts prepared to argue that the breed should be further divided into Laverack and Llewellin Setters. Add to this the fact that there are some who contend that all the breeds should be split between show dogs and working dogs and it becomes clear that making any definitive statement as to the number of British pointing breeds is fraught with danger.Nevertheless, it is my intention to divide this chapter into four main subsections covering the Pointer, English Setter, Gordon Setter and Irish Setter respectively, with the Red and White Irish Setter included with, but clearly distinguished from, the Irish Setter.

There are breed standards for all pedigree dogs published by the Kennel Club of Great Britain, the American Kennel Club and the Federation Cynologique Internationale, but I do not propose to quote chapter and verse from them here. Apart from the matters of coat and colour there is not a great deal of difference between the standards for all the dogs we are considering, nor indeed for quite a few other dogs including some outside the gundog group. They do, after all, share a common heritage going right back to the original wolf. The standards are widely available for those who enjoy reading that sort of thing.

The Pointer

The Pointer is commonly, but wrongly, referred to as the 'English Pointer', the word 'English' generally being appended in order to distinguish it from one of the continental pointing breeds. In passing it is worth remarking that it is also not unusual to hear reference made to 'pointers' when the speaker is clearly alluding to one of the German Pointers. The use of the term 'Pointer' to refer only to the 'native' British version of the pointing family of dogs has an element of unspoken elitism about it as if stressing that there is a class divide between 'real' Pointers and those other dogs which point game and share a portion of the Pointer's name. The attitude contrasts strongly with that of the Irish who are proud to preface their native pointing breed with the name of its country.

Personally I have no problem with the use of the term English Pointer, though I recognise that it is not strictly correct, and throughout this book whenever I refer simply to a 'Pointer' it can be taken that the word 'English' is implied (but not used) in front of it. German, Italian, Spanish and other continental breeds will likewise be referred to by their 'correct' names.

The Pointers of today are generally accepted to have been developed from Spanish Pointers brought home by soldiers returning from the continent following the Peace of Utrecht in the early eighteenth century. (For those of you who, like me, may be a little hazy on the subject the Peace of Utrecht was signed in 1713 and brought an end to the eleven years of bloodshed in what was known as The War of Spanish Succession. I am sure you wanted to know that.) There are few contemporary portraits of these early imports, but those that do exist suggest that the Spanish Pointer was a much heavier dog than his descendants are today. There is no doubt that the original Spanish dogs were crossed and re-crossed with other breeds, certainly including setters, foxhounds and greyhounds and possibly including bloodhound and even terriers in order to improve their stamina, pace, nose, determination or appearance. Some of these outcrosses are well-documented, most notably that where Colonel Thornton (1757–1823) mated a pointer bitch to a foxhound. Such a cross would probably not have been especially remarkable, but what distinguished this particular mix was that one of the pups, a dog called 'Dash', proved to be an exceptionally talented worker. It is also worth noting that, according to

A Pointer solidly on point on a covey of grouse.

contemporary accounts, despite being a superb dog himself, Dash never sired any offspring that came even close to matching his ability.

It is impossible at two hundred years remove to say with any certainty what combination of blood was instrumental in moulding the Spanish Pointer of the early eighteenth century into the Pointer that we have today. Even a mere fifty or so years after Colonel Thornton crossed pointer and foxhound to produce the celebrated Dash 'Stonehenge' in his excellent book *The Dog in Health and Disease* was reluctant to commit himself too strongly as regards the foundations of the breed.

> *The Modern English Pointer – It is possible that this comparatively light and elegant animal has been produced by careful selection from the original Spanish Pointer above described, but it is more probable that in all cases a cross directly with the greyhound, or indirectly with that breed through the foxhound, has been resorted to. In any case, the result is a dog still pointing steadily, and, in many cases, with true cataleptic rigidity, but showing the pace and endurance of the foxhound, and indeed being almost as fast as a slow greyhound.*

It is not difficult to follow the logic of those old sportsmen as they mixed and matched their breeds in order to get, eventually, to the combination of pace, endurance, nose and steadiness that they wanted from their pointers. Take the Spanish Pointer for the basic, pointing instinct, add the greyhound for pace and the foxhound for endurance. Ideally they would have ended up with a dog that combined the pace of the greyhound with the stamina of the foxhound and the nose and staunchness of the Spanish Pointer. In practice, there must have been some progeny that combined the pace of the Spanish Pointer with the nose and stamina of the greyhound and the staunchness on point of a foxhound.

Even today it is not unusual for an enthusiast to cross a Pointer from show lines with one from a working strain with the objective of producing offspring that have the looks to win in the show ring and the ability work in the field. And if such a mating should produce a dog with the appearance of a Show Champion and the working ability of a Field Trial Champion, then the proud owner would really have something to boast about. The problem is that it is just as likely that they will end up with a dog that looks like a working dog but has the working ability of a show dog: a combination that was hardly the result desired at the outset.

It must be remembered though that in the early part of the eighteenth century breeders tended to be much less sentimental about their animals than is the case today. You chose your dam and sire, mated them and, if the offspring didn't come up to expectations, you culled them and started again. It was an attitude that would not be acceptable to most people today, but there is no doubt that it produced results – provided the person organising the matings and assessing the potential of the outcome actually had the ability to judge, objectively, whether the experiment had been a success.

But however convoluted his family tree, the Pointer, very much as we know him today, was established and working on moorland and stubble from the beginning of the eighteenth century onwards. Contemporary paintings and etchings show dogs very similar to the modern Pointer in size and conformation. This is hardly surprising. The job that those early Pointers were bred to do has hardly changed from those days right up to the twenty-first century. The gun has come on a long way from the early flintlock, and shooting over pointing dogs is no longer the sport of choice for the vast majority who go shooting, but where pointing dogs are still worked on partridge or grouse the requirements of the dog are almost exactly the same as they were two hundred years ago.

I say 'almost' because today's pointers and setters are not usually expected to retrieve shot game, though back when practically all shooting was done over birddogs retrieving was considered a normal and natural part of their work. Today it is not unusual to hear the assertion, often made with great authority, that 'pointers and/or setters don't/can't/won't retrieve.' This is, quite simply, hogwash. Pointers and setters can and do retrieve. It is true that many working pointers and setters are not required to retrieve, and that in the interests of steadiness a lot of those who train and work birddogs prefer them not to be used as retrievers. But it does not follow that because a pointer or a setter is not asked to retrieve that he is not capable of retrieving.

But back to the Pointer in particular. He is most readily distinguished from the setters by the nature of his coat. Pointers should have a short, smooth, hard coat quite unlike the long, soft feathery coat of the setters. The usual colours are liver and white, black and white, orange and white or lemon and white, though occasionally there are solid coloured dogs, particularly black, and the breed standard allows for tri-colours as well. Height at the shoulder should be within an inch or two of two feet and the overall look of the dog should be that of a strong, lean, purposeful athlete combining speed and stamina with style and grace in its movement.

The short coat is often said to make the Pointer more suitable than the various setter breeds when working on hot summer days on the grouse moors. While this sounds good in theory, in practice I have never seen any signs that setters suffered more in the heat than Pointers. However: the opposite often is true, and I have seen a good few Pointers that were decidedly unhappy when they were out on cold, and more particularly, wet days. We had one Pointer that

This Pointer has found a pair of birds during a grouse count.

hated the wet so much that Georgina used to take her own coat off in order to protect him from the rain if there was a shower when he was on the hill. I had better add that Ferdy was a particular favourite, and thus enjoyed treatment that would have been denied most of our other Pointers, no matter how cold and wet the day, nor how much they shivered and shook and tried to look pathetic. But, special treatment for favourites aside, it is a fact that setters are better equipped for cold and wet than is the Pointer. That said though it is also fair to state that I have owned several Pointers that seemed to be quite impervious to the weather.

Temperament obviously differs from dog to dog, and it is unsafe to generalise about any breed. Even so, I would say that, as a general rule, Pointers tend to take a serious attitude to their work. I am not suggesting that they don't enjoy their work. Nothing could be further from the truth. Some do though, bring a single-minded purposefulness to their work that is less evident in, say, the rollicking, fun-loving Irish Setter. I don't mean to suggest that either attitude is a fault, either in the Pointer or the Irish Setter: merely to say that there are different ways of approaching the same job, and that the Pointer's way is sometimes more down to earth than that of his setter cousins.

It has also been my own experience that Pointers – or at least, some Pointers – are much more aloof than the setters: certainly than the Irish Setter. Where our setters have always been demonstrative and out-going; always ready to be fussed and petted; the Pointers have often seemed more remote: less willing to give or receive the sort of affection that the setters demanded at every turn. They have never been in any way aggressive. It has simply been a certain independence and standoffishness that is almost reminiscent of a feline rather than a canine nature.

This independent nature is also often evident when it comes to general obedience. A well-trained Labrador appears to obey its handler automatically, as if it accepts and enjoys the role of junior partner in the relationship. There is a sort of 'it pleases me because it pleases you' attitude to work combined with a reasonable certainty that if you blow the drop whistle or give the recall signal then the dog will do what you require – *and genuinely enjoy doing it.* With a working Pointer it often seems as if the dog/master relationship is more of a meeting of equals with the dog reserving the right to chose how, when and even whether, it will obey your commands.

I am not suggesting that Pointers are exceptionally bloody-minded, nor particularly difficult to train. It is more that they look on you as a partner rather than a master, and sometimes reserve the right to act independently rather than slavishly following the party line. There are times when this can be infuriating, particularly when 'acting independently' means slipping off to spend an hour or two self-hunting. Equally, there have been lots of times when one of the dogs has suddenly, and for no apparent reason, decided to extend the distance he is casting and ignore the turn whistle as he gets a hundred yards or so further out than I want him, then, just as I am about to abandon the whistle and scream at him to 'Get back here,' has banged on to point on a covey of grouse. A 'properly trained' dog would have obeyed that turn whistle. But then: with a 'properly trained' dog that would have been a covey that was simply not found, and a chance of a shot that the guns never knew they had missed.

The English Setter

The English Setter shares common antecedents with both the Gordon and Irish Setters, though the three breeds are now sufficiently well differentiated in their appearance for there to be little danger of confusing them on sight. The English Setter has the typical, long, silky setter coat, normally a mixture of white with black, brown, orange or lemon, or a combination of three of these colours. Feathering on the legs, tail and body contribute much to the dog's handsome

This predominantly white English Setter won the Champion Stake.

appearance, though in some show strains the feathering is so long as to render the dog almost useless for working in deep heather or rough cover.

His temperament should be gentle, friendly and a little less exuberant than the Irish or Gordon Setter, though as usual it is dangerous to generalise about the behaviour of any kind of dog. There can be wild English Setters just as there are quiet and reserved Irish Setters, but neither is typical of their breed. All setters are undoubtedly descended from spaniels, though with what mixture of blood from the old Spanish Pointer and from some or all of the various out-crosses that have gone into the final version of the modern Pointer is a matter for speculation. Stonehenge, writing in 1859, had no doubt about the origins of the setters.

> *That the setter is a spaniel taught by art to point his game is universally admitted, and Daniel in his 'Rural Sports' gives a copy of a bond signed by John Harris on October 7, 1485, in which he covenants to keep for six months and break a certain spaniel to 'set past ridges, pheasants and other game in consideration of ten shillings of lawful English money.' Thus it is certain that four hundred years ago the setting spaniel existed in this country, and most probably he was nearly identical with our modern setter, though probably not so fast.*

Until the latter half of the nineteenth century there were several different varieties of setter, all of which, excepting the Irish and Gordon, were merged under the blanket title of 'English Setter' when the Kennel Club categorised them in the 1870s. Twenty years earlier Stonehenge had listed several 'strains' of English Setter, including those of 'Mr Paul Hackett of Newcastle, Mr W Lort (the well known judge), Mr Wittington, Sir Bellingham Graham, and Mr Slatter.' That, far from comprehensive, list does not include the two best known breeders of that time, whose influence, and names are still celebrated today.

Two of Stonehenge's near contemporaries who were especially influential in the development of the English Setter were Edward Laverack and Purcell Llewellin. Indeed, in some countries both the Llewellin and the Laverack are treated almost as distinct breeds rather than as sub-divisions of the English Setter.

Laverack started 'his' line from a single pair of setters in about 1825 and claimed that he then bred them 'in and in' without any out-cross whatsoever. Those original dogs, named 'Ponto' and 'Old Moll' were supposedly obtained from the Rev. A. Harrison from near Carlisle who himself claimed to have kept his own breed 'pure for thirty-four years'. The wisdom of this very close in-breeding is debateable as Stonehenge pointed out at the time.

Unfortunately this close breeding produced a great many idiots and delicate constitutions, but if only a Laverack puppy had his senses, his limbs of good formation, and escaped the ills of teething, distemper, &c., he was sure to be a good dog in the field *when well broken, but he required a deal of this, being naturally wild and headstrong.*

Laverack bred setters for work and at that time 'work' meant serious shooting. Attitudes to working dogs were less sentimental and more practical in those days. Dogs were expected to work long and hard and any that did not measure up to the required standard were likely to get short shrift. This sort of regime may not be good for the individual dog – particularly for the individual with less than average working ability – but it undoubtedly promotes the rapid development of the breed.

An English Setter from proven working lines.

The primary task of a setter in the shooting field is to find game, and if he can do that without the need for constant handling then so much the better. The nineteenth century sportsman was interested in killing grouse or partridges: not in constantly blowing a whistle in order to keep his dog under control. But the growing popularity of field trials towards the end of the nineteenth century brought with it a demand for dogs that could be 'handled': that is to say, would turn and drop to a whistle and adjust their quartering according to the instructions given to them by the handler. Purcell Llewellin set about 'improving' the Laverack strain by breeding for this 'handleability' while retaining the drive, stamina, nose and field craft of the working Laveracks.

He was enormously successful in this endeavour and setters from the Llewellin lines have become the foundation of working and trialling kennels all over the world. When Laverack died in 1877 Llewellin took over his dogs and continued to enjoy great success at trials in Britain while in America and Canada dogs of his breeding were equally dominant. While Llewellin was willing to sell his dogs abroad he was less keen to allow his rivals in British field trials to get their hands on his bloodlines, presumably because he wanted to keep winning himself.

Among the setters the English Setter probably exhibits the greatest divide between the show types and the working strains. The show English Setter is unquestionably a handsome animal but mentally and physically he is generally ill equipped to undertake the work for which setters were originally bred and which they are still required to do if they are worked seriously. If your primary interest in setters is competing in the show ring then you must look to show stock for your dog. If you want to work your dog or run him in field trials then you should only consider a dog from proven working lines. And if you are one of the great majority of English Setter owners who keep their dog first and foremost as a pet then you can select your puppy from whoever you like. Beware though of confining a working-type setter in a town flat. All that pent-up energy is going to need some sort of outlet.

The Gordon Setter

The Gordon Setter is named for the Duke of Gordon who kept a kennel of setters at Gordon Castle in Banffshire during the eighteenth century. That much is certain. It is sometimes claimed that the foundation of the breed came about when a setter was crossed with a working collie but I have never seen any evidence to support this and doubt if there is any truth at all in the story. It is certainly possible that one of the Duke's setters may have been crossed with a collie, whether by accident or design, and might be that, rather like Colonel Thornton's pointer foxhound cross, the progeny were useful dogs, but to suggest that a single collie dog forms the foundation of the breed is to ignore all the known facts about the Duke of Gordon and his setters.

The modern Gordon Setter is a predominantly black dog with rich tan marking on the muzzle, legs and chest. A little bigger and heavier than either the Irish or English setters, he is nevertheless descended from the same genetic mixing pot and undoubtedly has his origins among those setting spaniels we met earlier in this chapter. There is some controversy as to whether the original Gordon Setters were black and tan, or black, white and tan, and this is not a matter on which it is easy to come to a considered judgement.

The Kennel Club applied the name 'Gordon Setter' to the breed in 1924. Before that they were known as black and tan setters, and were found in many kennels beside those of the Duke of Gordon. Indeed, there is plenty of evidence that the majority of the setters at Gordon Castle during the Duke's time were of the tri-coloured variety rather than black and tan only. Captain L. C. R. Cameron, writing the chapter on Gordon Setters in the Lonsdale Library edition of *Hounds and Dogs*, published in 1943 claims that the Gordon Setter was a solid black and tan dog and was known as a 'Gordon Setter' 'at least as early as 1746 and in all probability long before.' It must be said though, that his evidence is circumstantial and based on hearsay. Even so, he may well be correct in his assertion. Certainly Stonehenge, when writing in 1859 confirms the earlier use of 'Gordon Setter'

> *After a lengthy controversy, it is now generally admitted that the Gordon setter was originally white, black and tan, and that many black and tan setters were not descended from the Gordon Castle kennels. The classes for this breed are, therefore, not now defined as for* Gordon Setters, *but for* black and tan setters *whether Gordons or not, and this appears to be the most sensible plan.*

The modern Gordon Setter is almost invariably black and tan. The breed standard states that 'a white spot on the chest is allowed, but the smaller the better'. It seems that the Gordon, or his ancestors, may have gone full circle from being black and tan, to black, white and tan, and now back to black and tan again. When we consider the Irish Setter we will see that something similar occurred with this breed, though in the opposite direction as it were, the Irish going from red and white to solid red and then back to red and white in some cases. Perhaps in the not too distant future there will be a move towards establishing the Tri-coloured Gordon Setter as a separate breed?

The Gordon Setter was always a bigger and heavier dog than the other setter breeds and is renowned for his stamina in the shooting field. As a trialling dog the Gordon was considered to lack some of the pace and style of the Pointer, Irish Setter and English Setter, though today there is little to choose between the best dogs of any of the breeds when they are seen in competition. Modern field trials, because of the number of entries, do not, and can not, test the stamina of the dogs taking part, but reports of early trials back in the nineteenth century tend not to rate the Gordon Setter highly in terms of his pace and style, but generally acknowledge his staying power.

From a shooting point of view the dark colour of the Gordon Setter might seem like a handicap when it comes to spotting the dog on point out on the hill. There are conflicting views on this. G. T. Teasdale-Buckell, writing at the turn of the twentieth century said:

A classic point from a Gordon Setter that has been successful in the show ring as well as in field trial.s

It has been said that a black-and-tan is a bad colour to see on the moors, but this is not so. No sportsman would use a black coat for shooting, because it is more conspicuous than any other, and what is true of a man's coat is true of a dog's colour.

Contrast that with the views of Captain Cameron, writing some forty years later.

One highly probable reason why dogs of so dark a colour as the black-and-tan setters of the House of Gordon were selected for work in the Highlands at the period to which I have carried them back was the difficulty of distinguishing them when at work on the hill. Under the Lieutenancy of Huntly the Gordons had received charters of many forfeited lands which involved them in frequent and desperate feuds with the neighbouring Mackintoshes, Camerons and Murrays, especially. Although when clad in tartan the figure of a sportsman was indistinguishable at a reasonable distance against the heather and bracken-clad background, a white dog accompanying him would be at once discernible a long way off, while a black-and-tan dog would be unnoticed. In this way a Gordon shooting over disputed territory would have been less likely to attract the attention of some dispossessed clansman and so compelled to exchange his sport for a mortal combat.

So you can take your choice of reasons for the Gordon Setter being a black and tan dog. Either he was bred so because he would be conspicuous against the hill when he was working, or because he would blend in and be inconspicuous. I suspect that the real reason has more to do with fashion than with any practical purpose, though I can say from experience that a black dog does show up reasonably well on the hill: though not as well as one with some patches of white.

The Irish Setter

The Irish Setter, rather like his black and tan cousin, has changed colour over the centuries: or at least, fashion has changed in its definition of the 'correct' colour for an Irish, or Red Setter. During the early part of the nineteenth century Irish Setters were predominantly red and white. By the start of the twentieth century the majority were the familiar solid red colour and it was claimed (wrongly) by some 'experts' on the breed that any trace of white was a fault. Red and white setters still existed of course. Some enthusiasts continued to breed the red and white variety from choice, and pups with more or less white on them could turn up in litters bred from all-red parents. Fashion, as fashion does, swung full circle and, by the end of the twentieth century the Red and White Irish Setter was not only accepted as something more than a throwback, but had actually been accepted by the Kennel Club as a breed in its own right.

Ironically, it was undoubtedly the influence of the dog show that originally turned the Irish Setter from a red and white dog to a solid red one, and then promoted the red and white as a separate breed a century later. From the point of view of the sportsman there are clear advantages to having a red and white dog on the hill rather than a solid red, in that a dog with some white on him is much easier to see when he is on point. This may not seem much of an advantage if you have only seen dogs on flat, open moors in good, bright summer conditions. Come back in the autumn to a rough, haggy moor on a dank, misty day and you will quickly appreciate anything that makes it easier to spot a dark dog setting motionless among dark heather.

The Irish Setter is distinguished from his English and Scottish cousins by more than the shades of his coat. Descriptions of the Irish Setter abound with words like 'rollicking', 'exuberant', 'roistering', 'fun-loving', 'friendly' and also, it must be said, certain others such as

35

Billy and Penny Darragh with two top class working Irish Setters.

*The handsome
head of a red
and white
Irish Setter.*

'head-strong', 'wilful' and 'wild'. This lively, endearing and at times frustrating character has been part of the Irish Setter from very early days as Stonehenge points out. 'They are slashing goers, with heads and flags well up, and the latter lashed merrily in most cases....'

This out-going nature is very much part of the charm of the red dogs, and largely accounts for their popularity as pets and as exhibits in the show ring where they love an audience to entertain and accept the attention and admiration as their due. At work too, it is usually abundantly clear that an Irish Setter is thoroughly enjoying himself whether working on moor or stubble. They are largely impervious to the weather and ours have happily worked on in the cold and wet long after our Pointers have made it clear that they, at least, would much prefer to be curled up back in their kennels.

As with, particularly, the English Setter, there is a wide gap between the show bred and the working bred Irish Setter. Show influence tends to ease towards bigger, heavier dogs that lack the drive for working on the hill, while among Irish Setters from working stock a certain lack of size is not uncommon. A small animal with the energy, determination and stamina to run for miles, and hours on the hill is obviously a better shooting dog that a big handsome brute that looks wonderful but lacks the basic drive to get out and find birds. However if the working side of the breed is allowed to become too small they will lack the ability to cope with rough ground and long heather and still work a good beat.

Irish Setters are as much at home in the autumn stubbles as they are on the heather moors.

Irish Setters have a reputation for being too wild and head-strong to keep as pets. This stems in part at least from their rapid rise in popularity as house dogs during the sixties and seventies when many were purchased as pets by well-meaning, but misguided people who thought that a dog, bred for working and designed to run, could be left to its own devices all day long in a town flat and then given a short walk on a leash in the evening.

In his native country the Irish Setter was much used on snipe and woodcock as well as grouse and partridge and this may account in part for his lack of regard for cold, wet weather. Grouse and partridge are normally shot over dogs during the early part of their respective seasons because in both cases the coveys quickly become wilder as the young birds mature. Birds that would have lain well to a pointing dog in August and September can be as wild as hawks in October, by which time driving them is the only practical way to shoot. Woodcock and snipe though can be shot over birddogs right through the season, and it is likely that it is to this that the Irish Setter may owe much of his hardiness.

Devotees of the Irish Setter are wont to call attention to his superior stamina when compared to the other 'British' birddogs. Certainly an Irish Setter, given plenty of running to get him properly fit, is capable of some astounding feats of athletic endurance, but the same can also be said of the English and Gordon Setters and of the Pointer. Of the four, the Gordon Setter probably has the best claim to being bred specifically for stamina, but this must be balanced against the fact that early commentators invariably stressed the Gordon's slower pace and heavier build as well as his powers of endurance.

That concludes our brief look at the several breeds of 'British' pointing dogs. The Pointer, Gordon Setter, English Setter and Irish Setter are the cornerstones of the breeds, with the Irish Red and White Setter, the Llewellin Setter and the Laverack Setter also considered as separate entities in some quarters. All have their differences, both physically and temperamentally, but all share the same reason for their existence. They were developed over several centuries to find game and to indicate the presence of that game to their masters, but to hold back from flushing it until the net, the hawk or the man with the gun was ready. And that, is pretty much what we still require them to do today.

CHAPTER 4
Show, Work or Pet?

It's all up to you, be it show, work or pet,
They're Kennel Club registered, wormed by the vet,
Make wonderful gundogs,
Or lapdogs, and perfect for showing.
We can't promise they'll win in the field, or the ring,
But they've got the right breeding, and that's the main thing,
So thanks for the cheque:
Now we're sure you must want to be going.

David Hudson

The first recognised dog show was held in 1859 at Newcastle. The show was organised by a Mr R. Brailsford and there were classes only for setters and pointers. It is reasonable to assume that, since this was the first dog show, the pointers and setters that were entered were all working dogs and clearly, at that time, there can have been no divergence between 'working' and 'show' types. Now consider the situation just under fifty years later, when Mr Teasdale-Buckell was writing a chapter entitled 'Pointers and Setters' in his 1907 book *The Complete Shot.*

> The dog-show setters are most beautiful creatures, but the points on which they win here and in America are not the points that a sportsman requires.
>
> Slack loin is only a drawback at the shows but it stops a dog in work. A long refined head is a beauty at the shows, but it holds no brains that amount to anything. But worse than all this is the fact that the hunting instinct has lapsed in the show breeds. To be induced to range they must be excited. Now, in the truly bred pointer or setter you may start by repressing, go on by directing, and end by many 'dressings,' but you cannot weaken the hunting instinct, however you try to do it.
>
> It is not very wonderful that show-bred dogs cannot win field trials. To ask a breaker to educate them is a little worse than to turn Irish salmon into the Thames and expect them to come back there. When the last Thames salmon was killed the last instinct to return to the Thames vanished from Salmo Salar. You can no more get it back than you can make a field trial dog out of a show-bred one, or bring the dead instinct to life.

Bear in mind that Mr Teasdale-Buckell wrote those words in 1907: just forty-eight years after the first dog show took place. It must have taken a few years for the dog show to become established as a means to an end for the exhibitor rather than as a forum at which to compare and compete with dogs that were bred for work. And once the principle of breeding for looks alone rather than working ability allied to looks was established it must still have taken several canine generations for the divide between show dogs and working dogs to open up sufficiently for there to be a discernible gap.

After all, if all pointers and setters were working dogs prior to the advent of dog shows, then the earliest of the subsequent crosses, despite perhaps being intended to produce dogs primarily for the show bench, must have, by definition, been made between a dog and a bitch from working stock.

And yet, less than fifty years after the first dog show, a respected, intelligent and knowledgeable writer was lamenting the divide that had opened up between working dogs and those bred only for show. Now consider that virtually a full century has passed since then and that the time available for the showing and working sides of the breeds to diverge has increased by two hundred per cent. It is hardly surprising that there is a wide gap between pointers and setters bred for work and for trials, and those bred primarily for showing.

It is generally agreed that this split between working and showing types is a 'bad thing'. In an ideal world, the argument goes, working dogs would have the conformation to compete in the show ring, while show dogs would have the drive, stamina, pace and nose to work in the field. This general agreement tends to fall apart though if we look a little more closely at why the various parties involved consider the status quo to be undesirable.

A show judge, presented with a typical working pointer or setter would probably start out by regretting its lack of size when compared to show bred dogs of the same breed. There is no doubt that a slightly bigger than average dog can stand out from the rest in the show ring. Then, in the case of setters, the coat of the working dog is unlikely to compare with the flowing feathering found on the show specimen. Certain other characteristics that may be slightly exaggerated in the show dog include a dished muzzle, a sloping back line, a dark eye, a pronounced 'top knot' or occipital ridge, and particularly flowing movement may also be lacking in the worker. The show setter or pointer is unquestionably a supremely handsome specimen and the average working dog does pale in comparison.

This working Irish Setter is smaller but much more mobile than its cousins from show ring stock.

The most important thing in a working pointer or setter is the dog's ability to produce game for the gums.

But now let us take one of those good-looking show dogs out onto the hill. If we are on a typical dogging moor there are going to be a few grouse out there somewhere, but there is going to be an awful lot of hill and heather between coveys. Which means that our dog is going to have to cover an awful lot of ground in order to find them. And because we humans tend to lack patience, we are going to expect him to get out and find them pretty quickly. So he is going to have to be capable of running fast and far over some possibly rough ground and he is going to need stamina to keep on running for several hours per day. And when his legs do take him into the vicinity of some grouse he will have to have a nose that is good enough to tell him they are there while he is still far enough back to avoid flushing them. The problem is that when he is in a show ring, there is no way that the judge can assess his pace, his stamina or the quality of his nose.

On the hill though it doesn't matter a damn whether the dog has a dished muzzle, a pronounced stop, or a dark eye. What matters is whether he can find grouse: how well he can cover the ground: how long he can work before he has to be rested: how steady he is on point and how clever he is at working out his points. The guns will gladly overlook a certain lack of size, perhaps a plain head, a dearth of feathering and even a light eye or a bad tail carriage – provided that the dog finds birds, points them, holds his point and then produces them for the gun.So show breeders concentrate on producing dogs with those characteristics that win in the ring, while those who trial or work their dogs (and there is a subtle difference) pick their sires and dams with a slightly different objective in mind. It may not be ideal, but then, we don't live in an ideal world.

Show

Let me start out here by declaring an interest: or, to be strictly correct, something of a lack of interest. Dog shows are not exactly among the activities that rate highly on my 'must do' list. It isn't that I haven't tried. There was a time, when Georgina and I owned our first Irish Setter, that I spent a fair few of my leisure hours at dog shows. Exemption shows, little local shows, Limit shows, Open shows, Championship shows: we did the lot, and Simon, who was a consummate showman, took his fair share of prizes. We made a lot of friends around the show circuit and some of them are still friends today, almost thirty years later. I have nothing whatsoever against dog shows, as such: it is just that they don't have any great appeal to me as a way to spend my time off.

But you may feel differently. If so you are in very good company, because the show dog 'industry' is very big business indeed, and thousands upon thousands of owners enter their dogs in shows, week in, week out, and thoroughly enjoy the whole scene. There are quite a few magazines devoted entirely to dog shows: the annual Crufts extravaganza gets prime time television coverage every year, and puppies from proven show stock change hands for very big money indeed. More importantly, there are several thousand exhibitors who get a great deal of fun out of their hobby: whether it involves travelling the length and breadth of the country in search of challenge certificates and champion status, or simply collecting rosettes from shows in the local village halls.

Showing a dog is a fairly simple procedure when compared to working one in the field or running him in a trial. For a start you and the dog are attached to one another by a lead during the whole time he is being judged. There are three stages to judging. First you 'stand' your dog in a line-up with the other competitors, which means you pose him in the approved manner for the breed, usually with one hand gripping his tail and the other one holding his chin in order to show him off at his best. Then the judge comes along and inspects the dogs individually: pokes, prods and counts their teeth and certain other bits before moving on to the third stage. This involves running the dog up and down the show ring so that the judge can assess his

These Irish Setters seem to reflect my own enthusiasm for the show circuit, though many owners do take great delight in showing their dogs.

42

movement. Then you all line up again and the judge 'pulls out' the winners to the centre of the ring, and you collect your rosette, or not, as the case may be.

And then next week, you do it all again, quite possibly with exactly the same dozen, or fifty or several hundred other dogs taking part. Except – and this is where dog shows and I begin to go our separate ways – the dog that won last week may get thrown out with the rubbish this week. And the winner may be one that the judge dismissed with no more than a glance last week.

In some ways this is a good thing, because it keeps hopeful owners coming back week after week to show their dogs. Not winning this week doesn't mean that you won't win next week. Or the week after that. The problem is: how can one expert in your particular breed assess your dog against the official breed standard one week, and decide that he is the best of the bunch, when another, equally eminent expert can look at him next week and consider him not worthy of even a Very Highly Commended?

My personal nadir as far as dog shows went occurred at a field trial, many years ago. A friend had a Pointer bitch on a lead, and he burst out laughing when he saw me looking at her. The reason was that, although the bitch had a lovely head and shoulders she was extremely long in the back and terminated in Queen Anne legs at the rear end. If you or I had entered her in the Pointer classes at a show we would almost certainly have been told – in the nicest possible way – that we were wasting our time showing her 'with that long back and those hind legs'.

But the owner wasn't you or me, but one of the better-known show judges of the time. And the reason that the bitch was at the trial was to try and qualify for the 'Champion' title that is awarded to Show Champions that can demonstrate a certain amount of ability in the field. That bitch had been awarded a challenge certificate by no less than five different championship show judges. Each one of them had compared and contrasted her with two hundred or more other Pointers and decided that she – bow legs, long back and all – was the very best specimen of the lot.

She went on to gain her Champion status, and did it the hard way by getting an award in open competition rather than running as a 'qualifier', which can mean no more than cantering about the hill and stumbling over a covey of grouse. And she was a lovely dog in many ways as well as being not a bad worker. But I can never think of her without feeling sorry for all the other competitors at those five championship shows who had paid their money and travelled from all over the country in order to have their dogs judged fairly and honestly and who had been let down by a system that is, at times, guilty of judging the wrong end of the lead.

Anyone who has had much involvement with the show circuit can regale you with a dozen similar stories. But even with that knowledge, thousands and thousands of hopefuls do set out with their dogs, show after show, travelling all over the country and spending a small fortune on entry fees, in the hope that this week it will be little Phred's turn to catch the judge's eye and collect the silverware. I suppose if all judging was strictly objective and followed the breed standard to the letter the same dogs would win every time. And while that would be great if you owned the winner, it would be a bit of a downer if you were one of the also-rans. It must be that element of uncertainty that keeps the enthusiasts going back time and again. And as long as they are enjoying themselves there is no reason on earth why they should not.

If, despite my personal reservations, you fancy getting a pointer or setter for the show ring, then the best place for you to start looking for a puppy is around the dog show circuit. Go along to a few shows – there are several magazines that will give you dates and times for shows and let you know whether there are classes for the particular breed you favour – and watch the classes: talk to the exhibitors and generally get a feel for the show scene. If you still want to take part after you have attended a few shows and met your future competitors you should have no problem finding someone with pups for sale of the type you want.

While there can obviously be no guarantee that the pup you buy will win in the show ring, there is no doubt that you are most likely to get a winning show dog from winning show parents. If you have been around a few shows, made friends with some of the breeders, and picked up the show jargon then when you come to buy a puppy the seller will be conscious of the need to try and sell you one that doesn't have any obvious faults. No breeder wants to see a dog with an undershot jaw, or bad movement, or some other fault being exhibited week after week with their Kennel Club prefix in the catalogue. If you show you are likely to be serious about showing before you buy your pup then a responsible breeder will be happy to give you as much help as they can in picking a good'un. After that, it's pretty much down to you, and what the judges think of little Phred.

And if at first you don't succeed… Well: keep on trying. If my cynical little mind is right, and half the requirement for winning in the show ring is how well known the person is at the other end of the lead, then the more often you turn up the better your chances of winning.

Work

Before we get too deeply into what constitutes a working pointer or setter we should perhaps begin by defining the word 'work' as it is applied to this particular branch of gundogs. Obviously a working birddog has to be one that is employed in the shooting field. But such a simple definition raises more questions than it answers.

If you live on a grouse moor and keep a kennel of pointers or setters specifically to shoot over during August, September and October, then you unquestionably have working gundogs. And even if you are not actually domiciled among the heather, if you keep dogs to go out regularly to find and point game for guns then yes: you have working birddogs. The word 'point' is important, because if your pointer or setter is not used to point game then it is not being used as a birddog. And what if you only take your dog out shooting once or twice a year? What if you run in field trials but never actually have birds shot over the dog? Does that still qualify your dog as a working dog?

I expect that whether you get a 'yes' or a 'no' to that last question would depend very much on whom you asked. Field triallers – even those who may only take part in one or two stakes per year – would probably give you an unqualified 'yes'. A gamekeeper from the Highlands, responsible for training and handling ten or a dozen dogs and working them for shooting parties five days a week from August onwards might be less willing to award the soubriquet of 'working dog' to any pointer or setter that wasn't practically a full-time professional.

Perhaps you spend a lot of time in July and early August out on the hills doing grouse counts. Performing this valuable service certainly counts as working your dog, though you will obviously not be shooting over him at that time of year. Then there are those pointers or setters that are worked as part of the beating line on driven shoots. This is not a practice that any trainer of birddogs would recommend, but it happens, and for some owners this as close to proper work as they are ever going to get. It certainly isn't pointer and setter work, but if it is all that is available, and if dog and owner both enjoy it, then why should they not do it? (I could give you several reasons why not if the owner's intention was subsequently to work the dog in its proper role as a pointing dog, but we will assume that is not the case.)

For the purposes of this book let us consider a pointer or setter to be a working dog if he is used for a purpose to find and point game: whether that game be grouse, partridge, woodcock, snipe, pheasant, ptarmigan, blackgame, or even something more exotic such as the corncrake. Not, I should add, that anyone would shoot a corncrake, but I have heard of pointing dogs being used by scientists studying these birds. I say 'for a purpose' because any pointer or setter will find and point game, if there is any game to be found and pointed, even if he is only out

Grouse counting can be a valuable service to moorland shoots as well as providing work and training for your dogs.

for a stroll round the park. As to the purpose: well shooting is the obvious one, plus field trials, grouse counts and even scientific research if you happen to be involved in such a thing.

Pointers and setters are rather different from most of the other gundog breeds in that they are not normally capable of putting in a full working day on their own. Because of the pace at which they work, the distances they cover and the type of ground they run over, it is usual to work a team of birddogs rather than a single individual, with the dogs taking turn and turn about through the day. This means that, if you want to work your pointer or setter in his proper role on the grouse moors, then you will need not one, but three or four pointing dogs to make up a team. Once you start to consider having a spare dog or two to cover for injuries or bitches in season, plus somewhere about the place a couple of old dogs that have retired and a puppy and a young dog 'coming on', then you will see that getting serious about working birddogs can mean you end up with something of a kennel full.

That particular scenario only applies if you want to go out and work a full team of dogs for a shooting party. If your interest is in competing in field trials then a single dog is all you need. The same can apply to grouse counting, where the keeper or moor owner is probably more interested in getting 'a feel' for the numbers of grouse on the ground rather than putting in a full six or eight hour day and covering the whole of several thousand acres. And of course, you may be able to team up with another handler or two in order to have enough dogs available for a full working team.

If you want a pointer or setter to work, or for trialling, then the opposite applies to the advice I offered for the potential purchaser of a show dog. If you want a dog to work, then it is essential that you get one from working bloodlines. This applies to practically every breed of gundog, not only to pointers and setters. Remember that the fact that the advertisement says 'Show, Work or Pet' does not ensure that the puppies on offer are really from working stock. In fact, I would suggest that in ninety-nine per cent of cases such an advert would practically guarantee that the pups were not the product of working parents in any real sense of the word 'working'. Pointers or setters that are capable of winning in the show ring and turning in a proper day's work on the hill are rare creatures indeed.

One of the problems of working pointers and setters is the relatively short 'window' in which their services are required. Grouse shooting in Britain starts on 12 August and continues until 10 December, but after the first few weeks of the season the birds are usually too wild to sit tightly enough for shooting over dogs. The working year, for many birddogs, involves a frantic few weeks of activity: getting fit by grouse counting at the end of July, shooting in August and early September, then back into the kennel for ten months rest until the next season comes round.

The season may be short but it is usually quite intense. For a few weeks in late summer you may be

Pointer and setter work calls for a team of dogs. Falconer Stephen Franks at a spring field trial.

able to work your dogs every single day – Sundays excepted of course – or for as many days as their fitness and your holiday entitlement will allow. Then quite abruptly, the time for shooting over dogs is over and there is nothing for them to do except eat and sleep. By comparison the spaniel or retriever handler can look forward to a season stretching over half the year. Starting on the grouse moors in August, then partridge and pheasant from September through to the end of January, there is work available for a good beating or picking-up dog month after month.

The working season for birddogs can be extended if you are interested in competition, with field trials being run in the spring, summer and autumn. And there are some keen sportsmen who enjoy the challenge of shooting over dogs right through the season despite the difficulty of getting close to the grouse from October onwards. Indeed, it is arguable that the most challenging sport to be had on the hill, requiring the very best from both guns and dogs, is to go grouse shooting over dogs in October, November and even December.

If you have the time, access to ground for training your dogs, kennel space for a full team and are fit enough for long days on rough ground, then there is nothing in the shooting calendar to match the thrill of working pointers and setters on the moors. Be warned though, that it takes a lot of commitment and a great deal of hard work in order to enjoy a few days on the hill each August.

Pet

It is a fact that, although most of the books and articles that you are likely to read about pointers and setters will be primarily concerned with them as either show dogs or working/trialling dogs, the great majority of the dogs themselves will be household pets and never see the inside of a show ring nor the smell the heather on a grouse moor. However, it is also true that quite a few of those working and show dogs also started out with owners who thought they were just getting a pet but progressed from there to developing an interest in shooting, showing or competing in trials. Ownership of a pointer or setter may start out on a whim, but it can easily take over your life. I bought an Irish Setter puppy as a surprise present for Georgina over thirty years ago, and we have had setters and pointers ever since, moved to Scotland in order to work and train them, chose the location of our houses in order to accommodate them and spent countless hours training, working, exercising, feeding, trialling, photographing and writing about them. And given the choice I would do it all again.

Aside from any lifestyle changes that may or may not occur, if you are thinking of a pointer or setter as a pet the first thing you should do is to ask yourself whether one of the pointing

Pointers and setters need a lot of space for exercise and training. The author with Humphrey.

Georgina relaxing with an unusually quiet litter of pointer pups.

breeds really is the right pet for you. There are those who would question, with some justification, whether a pointer or setter is a suitable dog for a pet at all. With their boundless energy, sometimes mindless enthusiasm and capacity for covering vast amounts of ground in a very short space of time, they are certainly not suitable pets for anyone who lacks either the time to exercise them or the space in which to do it. Pointers and setters were bred to run and bred to hunt: they were not bred to lounge decoratively around a seventeenth storey flat in the middle of a city.

That said, there are many thousands of pet pointers and setters belonging to happy owners who would not consider changing them for any other breed. They can and do make delightful and loving companions; they are mostly gentle despite their boisterous nature and particularly as regards Irish Setters tend to think the whole world is their friend. We have kept both Irish Setters and Pointers for over thirty years, and though we have shown them, worked them and run them in field trials, for most of that time we have kept them primarily as pets. It may seem a little strange then if I spend the next few sentences suggesting that, as dogs go, pointers and setters are probably not the best of breeds to select if you want a dog solely as a pet.

The pointing breeds were developed to meet a particular requirement of the sportsmen of the eighteenth and nineteenth centuries. Back then, before the days when pheasants were reared and released in vast numbers, grouse and partridge were the main quarries of the shooting man. These were wild birds, and not as amenable to management as today's pheasants. If you wanted to shoot them you had to go out and find them, and in order to do that you needed a dog that could cover a lot of ground in a short time and keep right on doing it. When birds were scarce the dog had to have the drive and the enthusiasm to carry on working plus the stamina to run for mile after mile at high speed. And because those old sportsmen were very determined and very talented at breeding the dogs they wanted they developed dogs that had pace and drive and stamina in ample measure.

In modern times, when a pointing dog is something of a non-essential luxury for most shooting men, pointers and setters are rarely kept and worked under the conditions for which they were originally bred. But bringing one of them into the house, teaching it to fetch your slippers, sleep by the fire and walk quietly to heel (if you can) will not turn it from a birddog into a lapdog. He is still a dog bred to have enormous reserves of energy, a burning desire to get out and cover miles of ground and the build to do exactly that. He needs to run: to gallop about in wide open spaces: and if you don't have the time and the ground to allow him to give rein to these desires then it would probably be better for both you and the dog if you picked something a little less demanding as your pet.

Having sounded that warning it is fair to say that the very fact that pointers and setters, particularly Irish Setters, have been popular as pets for the past fifty years or more has resulted in some modification of their temperament. A dog that is kept as a pet, or as a show dog, and never expected to work in the shooting field has no need for much of the drive and determination that is essential in the shooting dog. Indeed, from the pet owner's point of view, a dog that is a little quieter, calmer and more tractable than a highly charged working animal is much to be preferred. With breeders selecting for good looks and a quiet temperament rather than for those traits that are required by the shooting man many modern setters and pointers are far better suited to the pet home than might have been the case half a century ago.

As a working pointer and setter owner I might be expected to deplore the trend towards breeding good-looking, sweet-natured dogs that are effectively useless if you ask them to perform the work for which they were originally developed. Taking a more pragmatic view though, I have to admit that the great majority of pointers and setters today are never going to be worked as birddogs. Provided those of us who want to work dogs can still find blood-lines

What could be more appealing than this Pointer puppy?

that retain the proper drive, stamina, nose and working instincts to hunt grouse and partridge, it doesn't really matter if the majority of breeders are looking for something different in their litters. Times change, and we have to change with them, and if there are thousands of people who want pointer or setter puppies as pets then it is surely better that they can get dogs that are suitable as pets rather than be left struggling to cope with dogs that have latent abilities that they will never be required to employ.

Buying a pointer or setter is rather like buying a new car. Before you decide what model to spend your money on you will have given some thought to the purpose for which you are going to use it. If you need something to accommodate a large family plus a large family dog then that Ferrari is hardly going to serve. A Land Rover might be ideal for off-roading but it's not the thing for nipping in and out of town traffic. The same applies to picking your new pup. If you are going to work him then you must buy a pup that has working bloodlines. If he is just to be a pet, then those working bloodlines are probably best avoided. And if you are planning a foray into the show ring, then be sure you purchase from show lines.

Whatever your choice – show, work or pet – once you have picked your puppy and brought him home you will need to think about training him. We will look at that in the next chapter.

CHAPTER 5
Training

'A bird dog,' the Old Man told me, 'is trained in the back yard. There ain't no way in the world you can teach him to smell; so you don't have to bother about that. There ain't no way in the world you can teach him bird sense; so there ain't any use worrying about that. All you can teach this dog is a little discipline, so that he can use his talents to the best advantage.'
The Old Man and the Boy Robert Ruark,
Henry Holt & Co. 1957

There are three stages to training a pointer or setter. The first is to teach him the basic good manners that any dog, working or pet, should have: coming when called, sitting to command and walking sensibly when on a lead. Next, if he is to be a working dog, he has to be taught to turn to his whistle, drop to command, to shot and to wing, and, possibly, to quarter his ground properly. And then he has to learn how to work. Note that there is a distinction between those things he has to be taught and those he has to learn. Robert Ruark's grandfather – the Old Man of his boyhood autobiography – was absolutely right. There are only a limited number of things you can teach a pointer or a setter. Once he has the basics the only way to progress further is for the dog to get out on the hill and start learning by experience.

Working a pointer or setter is a partnership between you and the dog.

Every puppy is an individual and must be treated as such when being trained.

Before we go any further though it is important to understand that just because you don't have very much to teach your new pup it doesn't follow that training a pointer or setter is easy. Simple possibly, but easy? Almost certainly not. Other gundogs such as the Labrador may have to be schooled in the finer points of send aways and sitting deliveries, blind retrieves and sits and stays, but I can almost guarantee that training a Labrador will be a far easier task than educating a pointer or setter. It is all a matter of temperament.

Some dogs, and let us take our hypothetical Labrador as a typical example, are only too anxious to please. If you are happy then they are happy, and they will go to great lengths to try and please you. The typical pointer or setter is also anxious to please, but in this case it is more likely that they will be trying to please themselves rather than trying to please you. The trick is to try and ensure that the end product of your training is a dog that, in pleasing himself will also be pleasing you.

As always, when discussing the characteristics of breeds of dogs, we can only generalise. Although I have chosen a Labrador as my archetypal 'eager to please the master' dog, I have known one or two Labs that were as thrawn, hotheaded and virtually uncontrollable as any dogs I have ever seen. Whether this was entirely due to their breeding, or whether it was at least partly due to their upbringing I cannot say, though I suspect that in the worst cases it was due to a combination of circumstances that resulted in a naturally wild dog finding a home with someone who was severely lacking in the will and the ability to train and handle a dog.

I have also seen setters and pointers that were models of decorum, never put a paw out of place and lived only to satisfy every whim of their owners. However, I should make it clear at this point that I have seen very few really wild Labradors and hardly any setters of the Goody-Two-Shoes stamp. Your pointer or setter puppy may turn out to be a perfect little angel, but if I were a betting man I would be putting my money on a different outcome. A certain independence of spirit, coupled to a degree of wildness is only to be expected from a dog that has been bred, over several centuries, to run hard and wide and to work largely on his own initiative.

A good retriever needs to be calm, controlled and handleable. He is expected to sit quietly beside you at your peg while you rain pheasants down all around him. When a bird drops three fields away and he hasn't seen it you want to be able to handle him right out to the fall. He must be responsive to your whistle and ready to search the ground to which you direct him. There will be occasions when you see where a shot bird lands and the dog is unsighted, and you need to send him back, left or right until he is in the right spot to start hunting.

In direct contrast, a birddog has to go out and find game with very little, if any, help or guidance from his handler. Okay: so you may want to have a measure of control over his quartering, and you certainly should be able to decide the limits of the beat he is working: but when it comes to actually finding birds the dog is on his own. If you knew where the birds were you wouldn't need the dog. And where game is scarce – and places where game is scarce are exactly the sort of spots where pointers and setters are at their most useful – we need our dogs to run, and run, and keep on running despite the fact that there is little or no scent to keep them interested. To work as hard as we expect them to do, our pointers and setters have to be self-motivated. No dog would run as far and as fast simply to please us. Pointers and setters work the way they do because they want to find game, not because we want them to find it.

But all that energy, drive and independence comes at a cost. Training and subsequently controlling a pointer or a setter is generally more difficult than training most other breeds of gundogs. Spaniel trainers may point out that keeping a hard-going Cocker under control can take a great deal of skill and patience, but at least a spaniel is – or should be – working pretty much under the eye of the handler. A pointer or setter can be two or three hundred yards – perhaps as much as a quarter of a mile – away from the handler and still be comfortably on his beat. If he suddenly decides to chase a hare, or take off to explore the next county, there is absolutely nothing you can do about it.

Working a pointer or a setter is very much a partnership between you and the dog. It has to be a partnership founded on trust and mutual respect. You cannot tether him down to stop him running in: you can't keep him at heel or only allow him to work ten yards from your feet. The whole *raison d'être* of a pointing dog is that it can be sent out to hunt well out of gunshot: that single-handedly it can work ten or twenty times the amount of ground that a flushing dog such as a spaniel can cover. If the price we pay for that ability is a certain amount of difficulty in training and a tendency for the pointing breeds to have freer spirits than some other gundogs, then so be it. Try to think of it as part of their charm.

Basic Training

Let us begin by going back to the origins of the dog. Research suggests that all dogs are descended from wolves, and though your new pup may not look very lupine deep down inside he still has the instincts of a wolf, and a wolf is a pack animal. His natural state is to be a member of a pack with a clearly defined hierarchy within that pack whereby one animal is the leader and the rest of the pack are subservient. I know that this is a very simplistic view, but it is near enough for our purpose. The important thing, right from the beginning, is to make sure that your pup knows his status within the pack. And that he doesn't think that he is the pack leader.

Unless you have bought yourself an exceptionally brash and confident puppy the chances are that he will be a little bit nervous and lacking in confidence when you first bring him home. He has just been taken away from his mother and his siblings, probably for the first time in his

Gordon Setter pup. You should aim to establish the right relationship between you and your dog from a very early age.

life, and he will be feeling lonely, worried and insecure. There will never be a better time to start gently letting him know that you set the rules from now on and that he obeys them. And if you have just taken possession of one of those hard-headed, ultra-confident pups that crop up from time to time, then it is even more important that you do not allow him to set his own agenda during the first few days and weeks you share each other's company.

I do not mean that you should start formal training with your seven or eight week old puppy. There is plenty of time for that when he is a little older and a lot more mature. What you can, and should, do at this early stage though is to ensure that he understands that there are things that he does, and things that he does not do, and that you decide what those things may be. It may be that you don't allow him to get up onto the furniture, or that he is only allowed to sleep on one particular armchair. When you feed him you could make him wait until you give him permission before he dives into his bowl. You may not allow him to beg at the table when you are having your meals or to just rush out when the door is opened instead of waiting to be told to 'get on'.

Of course, if he is a kennel dog then much of this is irrelevant, but it is just as important that you establish the correct relationship from the beginning. If the only real contact he has with you is when you open the kennel door two or three times a day and let him out to play in the yard, or to go for a run, or to put in his food bowl, then he is liable to turn into one very independently minded young dog. There are some trainers who might see this as a positive advantage when it comes to beginning the pup's formal education, arguing that such a dog is 'un-spoiled', and for the more competent and experienced trainer this may be correct, particularly for the professional handler who is taking on a young dog between six and eighteen months old. For the amateur trainer though, allowing a young pup to establish, in his own mind, some sort of dominance over his owner, is likely to be the kiss of death to ever achieving real control later in his life. So use the first few weeks after you get your new pup, not to start 'proper training' but to gently show him that you are the boss – or at least, that the boss is what you intend to be.

It is never too early to begin teaching him what the word 'sit,' means. All it takes is to place one hand under his chest and the other on his rump, gently lift up and push down with them respectively, while saying the word 'Sit.' He will sit because he won't have any choice in the matter, then you can pat him and tell him he's a good boy and slip off his lead, or let him get on with eating his dinner, or running about the garden or whatever he was about to do. You don't have to make a big production out of it, or expect him to sit on command within a day or two, but it shouldn't be too long before he starts to recognise the word 'sit' and suit his actions to it.

At this stage though he is probably not going to be consistent in obeying the word. Sitting when told will be fine when he is calm and concentrating on what you are saying to him, but he is less likely to obey if he is bursting to get off his lead for a run in the park, or bouncing about giving you an enthusiastic greeting when you come home from work in the evening. These are the very times when it is most important to ensure that he does sit – even just for a moment – if you have told him to do so. It can be argued that, since trying to get a young puppy to sit when he is leaping about in delight to greet you is likely to be very difficult, you may be better to wait until he has calmed down before giving a command. What you are trying to establish during these early days are that he does as he is told *every* time he is told, and not just when it suits him. You must be consistent. If he is allowed to pick and choose when he obeys you now the chances are that he will expect to pick and choose later on in life. Conversely, if the habit of obedience, albeit only over a few very simple things, is ingrained from the beginning, then you have a much better chance of turning out a reasonably obedient dog later on when training becomes more serious.

Pointers and setters are not noted for their willingness to walk on a slack lead.

When to start training a pointer or setter – or indeed, any other dog – is one of those questions that is frequently asked but almost impossible to answer to the satisfaction of the enquirer. The only sensible answer is 'When he's ready', and such a reply is of little practical help. It is though, impossible to say that a puppy will be ready to start training at six months, or nine months, or one year old, because the optimum age varies with individual puppies. Besides, for most trainers there isn't a particular day on which a pup's training can be said to begin, like a child attending school for the first time. Rather the initial quiet discipline of getting the pup to sit, to come when he is called and to walk on a lead should all be looked on as part of his training, putting down a foundation for the future.

The business of walking on a lead is not something that seems to come naturally to pointers or setters. Most puppies will fight the lead initially but quickly settle down to the idea of having a collar, chain or piece of rope round their necks and acting as a restraint. Most older dogs can be taught to walk to heel, or at least to walk on a lead without continually pulling, but this doesn't seem to apply to the pointer and setter breeds.

It is certainly not impossible to train pointers and setters to walk at heel or to trot along on a slack lead, but it is not usually easily accomplished. Go to a field trial and take note of how many of the dogs are straining at their leashes as they wait their turn to run: then consider that, as trial entrants, these are probably some of the best trained pointers and setters in the country. Pulling on the lead, or at least standing at all times at the full limit of the lead's travel, seems to be the default state of most pointers and setters.

Simon, the first Irish Setter that we owned was, typically, a dedicated puller. My wife Georgina took Simon to training classes and eventually reached the point at which he was competing in obedience events, but initially she used to do two laps of the room to everybody else's one because Simon simply dragged her around. With some help from the class tutor, a lovely man called Ben Johnson, sadly no longer with us, she managed to turn him into quite a well behaved dog – for a setter. It has to be said that Simon was a tremendous show off and loved having an audience. There were occasions when he won prizes for obedience, but with Simon there was always the possibility that, having retrieved his dummy as per specification, he would elect to toss it up in the air and catch it two or three times, then do a lap of honour around the obedience ring before returning to Georgina and executing the perfect sitting delivery. These performances were popular with said audience but didn't attract very high marks from the judges. Simon always enjoyed himself though, and as far as he was concerned that was why we were at the show in the first place.

I have been told on several occasions that it is best not to make a pointer or setter walk at heel, or on a slack lead, because it may inhibit them later on when they are expected to get out and hunt for game. This may even be true, but I suspect it is more likely to be an excuse proffered by trainers whose dogs are hauling away on their leads as if their very lives depended on it. I will even confess to having used it myself from time to time. I have heard of one trainer of pointers and setters, also no longer with us, who could go to the hill on a shooting day with a team of dogs and have one out working while the other three or four stayed quietly at heel with no need of a lead, couples, or any other form of restraint. I have no reason to doubt the truth of this, though I never witnessed it for myself, but I can say for certain that he must have been an exceptionally talented trainer and had a remarkable hold over his dogs.

So if you want your dog to walk properly, quietly and soberly at heel then it is almost certainly possible for you to train him to do so, but it may take quite a lot of time and effort when compared to some other breeds. I am most certainly not advocating that you allow your pup to heave and tug away in a completely unrestrained manner every time you put the lead around his neck, but I am saying that being connected to the dog by a fairly taut length of line is not uncommon even among the best trainers of pointers and setters. How insistent you are upon this particular aspect of discipline is pretty much up to you, but if your pup doesn't amble along at your heel like a well bred Labrador then you will not be alone among pointer and setter owners. In fact, you will actually be in some pretty good company.

If your pup is from show or pet lines rather than from working or trialling stock you may find that getting him to accept the basic disciplines such as walking on his lead without pulling will be relatively easy. Provided that you have got him for a pet, or as a show dog, then this is obviously something of a bonus. There is no great pleasure to be gained from having fifty pounds of bone and muscle tugging away at your arm every time you go out for a walk. There may be a payback later if your ambitions run towards shooting or field trials, where it is possible, though not certain, that your pup may lack some of the drive required of a working dog. Obviously, this is only going to be a problem if you plan to work your dog, and if you do, then you should have bought a pup from working parents in the first place.

Getting your pup to come to you when you call him can be the easiest, or sometimes the hardest, part of training him. In the house or in the garden, when there is nothing to distract him, the pup will probably rush up to you whenever you whistle or call his name. If you are out in the fields or in the park and there are exciting scents to be investigated, other people to befriend, small birds, rabbit or squirrels to chase, then it is hardly surprising if a young dog suddenly develops a deaf ear to your entreaties. How much of a problem this may be will depend on how much of a hurry you may be in, and what more serious problems are lurking in the neighbourhood.

There are several little tricks that may help to get your pup back to you. Continually shouting or blowing the whistle when he is obviously ignoring you is not one of them. All you are doing is teaching him that he can ignore the whistle if he chooses and no form of divine retribution is visited upon him. If you wait until he finally comes back and then chastise him you are simply adding to the problem because in his mind he will have been punished for coming back. All that this will do is to make him even more reluctant to return to you the next time he is running free.

Walking away and leaving him can often have the desired effect. As long as you are there in sight, or as long as he can hear you whistling or calling, he knows that you are around and that he can return to you whenever he is ready. If you go off and leave him there is a good chance that his confidence will evaporate and he will come running to see where you have gone at which point you can make a fuss of him and slip the lead around his neck. This is fine if he is running about somewhere safe. It is not such a good ploy if there is a main road, a field full of lambs, a keeper's release pen with a couple of thousand pheasant poults or something else of that nature in the vicinity. The answer to this, very obviously, is that you should never have let him run free there in the first place. I know that this will not be much comfort as you desperately try to get control of the little brute before the worst happens, so *think* before you take that lead off and let him away.

Getting down to his level can sometimes induce a reluctant runaway to come back. Squatting down and extending your arms in a welcoming fashion can persuade a pup to come back for a cuddle. In more pressing circumstances laying flat on the ground has been known to stimulate a pup's curiosity enough to bring him within range. Likewise, running away may make him decide that you are playing a game that he should join in with you. In some cases a stern voice may do the trick, but there is always the danger that it may have exactly the opposite to the desired effect. Some pups will be brought to heel by a touch of anger in your voice, but others will realise they are in trouble and become even more determined to stay out of reach. Bribes, such as biscuits, chocolate drops or bits of dried meat may work, making a fuss of another dog, if another dog is handily available, may induce a fit of jealousy. Throwing a ball for him to chase, or throwing something like his lead at the pup if he comes near enough, can also jerk him out of independence mode. It may never be a problem, or it may drive you mad, but in the end you just have to find out what works for you and your pup. Hopefully, later on when he is properly trained, the problem won't arise any more. But note that I said 'hopefully'. There are no certainties with pointers and setters.

Training Proper

By 'Training Proper' I mean training for work in the field, or in other words, training your young pointer or setter to do the job he was bred to do and work as a pointing dog. If you are looking for a show dog, or an obedience competition entrant then I should recommend you to some other publication specialising in those aspects of dog work, or possibly to your local dog training class. Indeed, attendance at dog training classes will benefit almost any young dog in terms of his socialising with other dogs and dog owners and will probably be useful for the novice trainer as well.

The first thing to decide, before you start training your puppy, is what it is you hope to produce at the end of his lessons. The trite answer, 'A trained dog', really doesn't suffice unless you have given some thought to exactly what it is you are training him to do. I am talking about whether you are setting your sights on field trialling, grouse shooting, low ground shooting, grouse counting or quite possibly, all of the above. Much of the training is in any case the same, whether you intend the dog for trials, for shooting or for the sort of non-combatant information

If you aim to compete in trials you must have a completely steady dog, like this Pointer.

gathering that grouse counting involves, but there is a definite difference in emphasis between the sort of work required by a shooting party and that required by field trial judges. We will be looking much more closely at both these requirements in later chapters, but it is important to realise that there are some, albeit slight, differences between 'shooting' and 'trialling' dogs and thus some slight differences in the way you approach their training.

Primarily a field trial prospect needs to be subject to rather more close control than a shooting dog. This is not to say that a shooting dog should run in an uncontrolled manner, but that a trialling dog is likely to be working more under the direct instruction of his handler and less on his own initiative than a shooting dog. Thus the trainer of a trialling dog should give more emphasis to rapid response to turn and drop whistle, to hand signals, to regular, even quartering of ground, to instant reaction to shot or to wing, to backing and to steadiness on point.

That sounds like pretty much the whole gamut of birddog education, so perhaps I should try to expand. Elimination can come very rapidly in the course of a stake where forty-plus dogs are being judged. If you are asked to stick to a particular boundary on your beat and your dog takes an extra dozen strides – let's say an extra thirty yards or so – before turning on his whistle he may well be eliminated for going off the beat. If he doesn't drop immediately when birds get up or when a shot is fired, or if he takes a step forward to see what is happening when a covey rises: if he fails to back his brace mate when the other dog points or has to be whistled at

Irish Setters at a field trial. The foundation of training for all dogs lies in basic obedience.

several times before you can pick him up: if he takes even one step in pursuit of a hare or a rabbit before turning off it: then he stands a very good chance of being 'of no further interest' to the judges.

A trial dog, even the dog that gets through both, or all three or even four rounds, and goes on to win the trial, is unlikely to be down under the judges for more than twenty minutes in the course of the trial. It may seem like a hell of a lot longer when you are handling him, but the sheer number of dogs to be judged ensures that it is not so. A working dog, as part of a team of three or four pointers or setters, is likely to be out on the hill for six or seven hours on a shoot day and thus may be actually working for two or three full hours or more. We tend to pick up our working dog 'next time he has a point' or 'when he starts to look tired' or just when it is convenient. During a trial, when the judges say 'Pick them up please' they mean right now, and the fact that your dog is just heading out towards one of the flanks doesn't mean you can do what you would do on a shoot day and wait until he has completed that side of his beat and bring him in as he crosses in front of you. It means drop him or turn him now, and then call him back and put the lead on. Right away.

A field trial dog has to be under the control of his handler if he is to have any realistic prospect of success. In complete contrast, if a birddog will remain steady on point long enough for the guns to come up to him, then it is possible to shoot over him even if he has had no training whatsoever. And practically all pointers and setters will point game because it is their very nature to do so. So, if we were to try and define the absolute minimum training that a pointer or setter needs before he can be considered as a shooting dog the answer would be, in many cases, none at all. Take one totally untrained dog out to the hill, turn him loose and let him go, and there is a very good chance that you will be able to shoot some grouse over him – if there are any grouse to shoot.

There is also a very good chance that he will run in when the birds rise, chase birds, rabbits, hares and possibly sheep, hunt wherever on the hill his inclination takes him and possibly disappear into the distance and only come back to you when he is tired and hungry. Let me make it quite clear that I am not recommending that you take a totally untrained dog out on a shooting day (though you would not be the first person to do exactly that). Rather I am trying to emphasise that the really vital elements of pointer and setter work – finding game, pointing it, and holding the point – are things that the dog will do all by himself. Our job, as trainers, is simply to overlay those natural instincts with a certain amount of discipline.

So what do we need to teach our pupil? If we break down our training requirements into their most basic elements we come down to just three things.

1 To come back to you when he is called/whistled.
2 To turn on command.
3 To drop (sit or lie down) on command.

If you have a dog that will do just those three things then you are well on the way to having a trained birddog. Other things such as quartering the ground properly, dropping to shot and to wing, backing and even holding steady when on point can all be taught by making use of those three basic disciplines.

This may have given you the impression that training a pointer or setter is an easy matter to accomplish. If so, think again. Training a pointer or setter may be simple, but there is no guarantee that it will be easy. Everything depends on the individual pupil and how you and the dog inter-react. Some dogs are indeed very easy to train, but it has to be said, that some are quite definitely not.

The basic principles of training pointers and setters are exactly the same as for training any other breed of dog.

Drop whistle at the ready as this young Pointer is clicked in to flush a covey of grouse.

Practically all birddogs will point: it is in their nature to do so.

1 You give a command, by voice, whistle or hand signal.
2 You make sure that the dog takes the appropriate action in response to the command.
3 You do it again, and again, and again until the dog obeys the command automatically.

The usual principles apply to training pointers and setters as they do to training any other dog. Keep each thing to be learned as simple as possible, and keep repeating the lesson until the response from the pupil is automatic. Reward him when he gets it right. Short lessons given regularly are more valuable than long lessons delivered occasionally. Keep the pupil interested and end the lesson when his interest starts to wane. Always try to end up on a high note. Never be tempted to rush things, or to go on to the next stage before the current lesson has been properly learned. Note that this does not mean that you should do nothing but 'sit' commands for hour after hour until you and your pup are both bored out of your minds. On the other hand, there is no point in trying to drop your pup in the middle of a recall unless he has pretty much mastered both the drop and recall commands already.

Every puppy is an individual and must be trained as such. What works with one pupil may not work with another, and it is up to you, as the pup's trainer, to assess your pupil's capabilities, character and capacity to learn and adjust your training regime accordingly.

The basic training can be done in your back garden, the local park, a handy field or even, at a pinch, in your living room. If you are a newcomer to the joys of training pointers or setters you might be well advised to sign up for evening classes in dog training if such a course is available locally. At this stage it doesn't matter whether you are interested in shooting, field trials, showing, or just getting a bit of control over the family pet: the principles are exactly the same and will stand you in good stead later when you move on to more advanced work.

The absolute basic training means getting your puppy used to walking on a lead, obeying the sit command and coming to you when you call him. If he isn't yet at this stage, then this is the place to start. Put him on his lead, walk him along a little way and then say 'Sit' and pull back on the lead while pressing down on his hips so that he sits down. Tell him he is a good boy, keep him sitting for a few moments, then say 'Get on' and start walking again. Do it again. And again. And again.

If you want him to walk to heel and not tug on his lead then this is the time to teach him that lesson, and I wish you the best of luck. Whether this is a simple task or something more akin to the labours of Hercules will depend on the breeding and temperament of your particular pup. The principle is simple enough: you keep tugging him back to the correct 'at heel' position while giving the command 'heel' and repeat the lesson until he realises that he is supposed to walk along without 'straining at the leash' all the time. He may learn this quite quickly. It is also possible that he may not – ever.

While we are on the subject of commands, it is entirely up to you what command you attach to each action. Where I use words like 'sit', and 'heel' and 'stay', and 'hup' you can substitute any alternative that takes your fancy: provided that you are consistent in its use. A command doesn't have to be a spoken word. It can be given via a whistle, a hand signal, a snap of the fingers or some other noise such as a hiss or a click of the tongue. All that matters is that the dog learns to associate that particular noise or movement with a particular action that he is required to carry out.

The basics of pointer and setter training can be taught in the back garden.

'Down' is the command normally used to instruct a dog to lie down, as opposed to sitting down. In pointer and setter circles the 'down' command is usually replaced by the word 'hup': said to derive from the old command of 'muzzles up', used in the days of muzzle-loading shotguns to let the other shooting gentlemen know that you were re-charging your weapon and therefore wanted the dogs to lie down and cease working until such time as you were ready to re-join the proceedings. It doesn't matter which command you use, provided you are consistent, as both 'down' and 'hup' are short, distinctive noises that cannot be easily confused by the dog or mistaken for something else. 'Hup' has the weight of tradition behind it, while 'down' is the logical word to use to get a dog to lie down.

Once the sit and/or the down command has been reasonably well installed in your pup's consciousness you can turn your attention to getting him to stay and then to come back to you when you call him. Getting him to stay initially is simply a matter of sitting him and then taking just one or two steps away from him while giving the command 'stay' and reinforcing it with your hand help up with the palm facing the pupil. If he doesn't leap to his feet and come after you as soon as you move away you can go back to him after just a couple of seconds and make a fuss of him. If he does follow you, take him back to where you had left him and sit him back down before trying again. All you are trying to do in the beginning is to get him to stay for a couple of seconds while you are no more than a couple of feet away from him. There will be plenty of time to extend both time and distance as he learns what is expected of him and realises that he is not being abandoned.

Commands can be spoken, whistled or signalled by hand. The handler is keeping the Pointer steady as the gun gets into position.

At first you should always go back to the pup at the end of his period of 'staying'. Only when he has mastered this discipline should you start calling him to you instead of you going back to him. Don't call him to you all the time even then, but mix up some recalls with times when you go back to where he is sitting. Squatting down so that you are at his level and extending your arms when you call him can be a big help in encouraging him to come to you. If he is reluctant to come to you, turning your back and running away from him will often bring a pup rushing up to join in the game. Making a fuss of him when he arrives should be automatic. Putting him on the lead straight away should not. If he finds his freedom is curtailed as soon as he comes to you he may decide to keep out of reach until he is ready to be put on his lead. Get him back, reward him, let him run off and come back again once or twice: then pick him up. Some pups can be greatly encouraged by giving them a little reward such as a biscuit or a sliver of dried meat when they get things right, and this can be particularly useful as a bribe when you are teaching him the recall.

How far you go beyond these basic lessons is your decision. If you are going to dog training classes you will probably be learning the basics of training for obedience competition. This includes the dog walking closely to heel both off and on the lead, distant control – getting the dog to sit, lie down and stand in response to commands when you are some distance away – retrieving a dummy, finding an object by recognising the owner's scent, teaching the dog to respond to hand signals sending him away from you or to the left or right, and staying for ten minutes when the handler is out of sight. If you and your pup enjoy the lessons and want to go on to a higher level of obedience work then it is likely to be highly beneficial to both of you.

If you are not interested in pursuing obedience work to its higher levels though you can simply concentrate on the basic lessons of sitting, staying and coming back when you call. Once the pup has got used to obeying voice commands and responding to your hand signals you can introduce whistle commands for the same actions. Teaching your pup to respond to the whistle is essential if you are planning to work him either in field trials or as a shooting dog. A whistle is quieter than a human voice and thus less likely to disturb game but at the same time it can be heard by a dog at much greater distances than a shout. It also has the advantage of being largely expressionless. If your dog is reluctant to return to you your voice will almost certainly reflect the annoyance that you are feeling and may well exacerbate the problem. Letting the pup know you are angry may bring him rushing back, but it is at least as likely to persuade him that he is better to keep well out of your way for the moment.

Every dog, not just pointers and setters, should be trained in the basic disciplines of coming to you when he is called, walking on a lead, sitting and staying when told. How much further you go then is up to you and will depend on what hopes and aspirations you may have for your pup. If these include working him, for field trials or in the shooting field, then you will have to go on to some more specific lessons, and we will be looking at those in the next chapter.

Pointers and setters must hunt for their game over vast areas and thus must work a great deal on their own initiative.

CHAPTER 6
Field Training

It would appear at first sight an impossible task to attempt to discuss in curtailed form the absorbing topic of the Training of a Gundog, but, on reflection, provided always the essentials are set forth, the advantages of generalising are not only obvious but may even be of the greater value.
The reason for so saying is that the uninitiated, who read an exhaustive treaty on the subject, say, of training a spaniel to a gun, are wont to follow the instructions too literally and think, to use a homely expression, that every dog can be whacked with the same stick – than which no greater error can be made.
Lieut.-Col. G. H. Badcock – writing in *Shooting by Moor, Field & Shore,*
The Lonsdale Library, 1929

Although it is over seventy years since Colonel Badcock wrote those words they are as true today as they were back then. Dogs differ: even two pups from the same litter can be complete opposites in their characters and their responses to training, and to try and set out rigid rules or routines for training any dog is to invite disaster for anyone who attempts to follow them. One dog may do instinctively and quite naturally something that another dog will require many lessons to master. In some cases it is possible to put hours of hard work into training a dog to perform a particular function only to produce, as an end result, a dog that is less useful than if the training had never been given in the first place.

It is possible to train a retriever to be wonderfully responsive to hand and whistle signals when it is sent to search for a shot bird. A good handler can send his dog out, back, to the left or to the right with superb precision, finally putting the dog right on the spot where he believes the bird is lying, and only then order it to start searching for the retrieve. There is no denying that such control is useful at times, but not when the dog has been so brain-washed into following orders that it loses the desire or the ability to get out and hunt on its own initiative. Then, when the inevitable happens and the shot bird is not lying exactly where the handler has marked it, the over trained dog is defeated. A little less training and a bit more encouragement to the dog to work on its own initiative might have produced a dog that would cast itself across the wind, then get its nose down and hunt for the missing bird instead of relying on the handler to 'find' the bird for him.

The concept should not be taken too far though. We are all familiar with the type of dog that works on natural ability alone with no input from the handler – or no input that is heeded. There is often quite a lot of whistling and shouting instructions to this type of dog, but usually very little notice is taken by the recipient. Too much training may be a fault, but it is not nearly so common a fault as the failure to train enough.

I have already touched on the subject of deciding what it is you want from your dog when you eventually start working or trialling him. Before getting too involved with training your pup for the field it is worth thinking this through. A field trial dog must be under control if he is to stand any chance of getting among the awards: a shooting dog really ought to be under control, but it isn't actually essential, provided he'll stop and point when he finds game. Pointers and setters are not normally thought of as retrieving dogs, but if you want to use one to retrieve as

Solidly on point and demonstrating the total concentration that the scent of game can induce in pointers and setters.

well as to find live game for you there is no reason why you should not. How much aptitude he will have for the task will depend on the individual dog. Once again, I should emphasise that I am not advocating taking an untrained dog into the shooting field. Working a well-behaved, responsive and obedient dog that you have trained yourself is a uniquely satisfying experience and infinitely better than spending the day trying to control some headstrong reprobate.

I am not going to try to set out a strict training programme for pointers and setters, because, as Colonel Badcock wrote so succinctly, it is probably better to generalise than to be to precise when it comes to writing about dog training. The important things are:

to keep lessons short and simple:
to discover what your dog responds to best, and then adapt your training methods to suit:
to take your time and not be tempted to rush on to the next stage too quickly:
to ensure that neither you nor your dog get bored with lessons:
and to always end a training session on a high note.

There are usually several ways of achieving the same result, and which one works best will depend on the individual temperaments of both you and your dog. It doesn't matter if he learns to quarter by being worked on a line, turned on a whistle, or being encouraged to chase you to and fro across a field provided that, eventually, he learns to quarter. If you are lucky with your pup he may even quarter naturally with only the minimum of encouragement and advice from you. It doesn't matter how you get there as long as you arrive eventually.

Equipment

Training a pointer or setter doesn't require much in the way of equipment. The only really essential item is a whistle, or perhaps two whistles: one for turning and recalling and one for dropping the dog. Some handlers combine the turn and recall whistle with the drop whistle, generally using a couple of short peeps to turn the dog, a longer series of short peeps to recall him, and a single, long blast to get him to drop. Others prefer a loud whistle such as the ACME Thunderer to give the drop signal, and there is a certain satisfaction in being able to give a really loud blast when your pup is chasing a hare or disappearing over the march. There is also a certain embarrassment when he completely ignores you, but hopefully that isn't going to happen to you. I don't know whether a loud blast is more effective than a quieter one in dissuading a dog from taking off in hot pursuit, but it certainly sounds to me as if it ought to be more effective. I can't speak for the dog though.

A check cord is not quite essential, but it is something that most pointer and setter trainers find useful. Thirty to fifty or yards of light but strong cord attached to a collar will enable you to maintain contact with your dog at a distance. If you do use a check cord then a pair of leather gloves is invaluable to prevent your hands from getting rope burns. It is definitely not a good idea to grab hold of a thin cord with your bare hands when one end of it is attached to an Irish Setter in full flow.

Mrs Julie Organ with her drop whistle ready to hand as she works out a point at an International Challenge Match held at Balmoral.

A check cord can be useful when teaching a young dog to quarter his ground.

I was once advised to fit a block of wood to the end of a check cord, the theory being that, instead of holding the cord in my hands I could let it run loose and then check the dog by standing on the cord and letting the block of wood get trapped against the side of my boot. The idea worked well – up to a point. The point at which it stopped working well was the moment when the block of wood, travelling at pointer speed Mach 1 and with the full weight of a Pointer dragging it along, hit my foot. The bruises went down after a week or so and I found a better use for the block of wood next time I lit a fire. It is not an experiment I have ever felt inclined to repeat.

The check cord is useful for turning the dog when he is learning to quarter and for steadying him from a distance when he is on point or backing another dog. Later in his training, when he is being allowed to run free, dragging a check cord behind will help to remind him that he is supposed to be working under orders and not just pleasing himself. I have known the odd dog that simply refused to run at all while dragging a line behind them, but most dogs either ignore it right from the beginning or quickly become accustomed to it.

Unless you are training your dog solely for falconry, or perhaps grouse counting, you will have to get him accustomed to gunfire at some stage in his career. This is usually less of a problem with pointers and setters than it can be with some other breeds, such as retrievers, because at the moment a gun is fired in the course of pointer and setter work the dog is totally occupied with the birds that it has just found, pointed and lifted. If you have a shotgun of your own it can obviously be used to get the dog used to the sound of shots. For those who don't have a shotgun certificate one alternative is to buy a starting pistol. The crack of one of these little pistols is not quite the same as the sound made by a shotgun, but they can be useful as a first introduction to gunfire. Alternatively, look for a friend who shoots and may be willing to spend a little time and a few cartridges helping you with your training. A few years ago I might have suggested buying a cheap shotgun just for training purposes, but in today's climate you might not be able to persuade your local police firearms department that this was a suitable reason for you to be granted a shotgun licence.

One other training aid that has become widely available in recent years is the electric collar, also called the training collar or something similar. This comprises a small, hand-held transmitter and a dog collar with a receiver and a device that will administer an electric shock to the dog that is wearing it when the button on the transmitter is pressed. They have a range of up to three hundred yards and the more sophisticated models can be set to give shocks of differing severity according to their setting.

All working and trialling dogs have to get used to hearing the sound of shots fired close to them during a shooting day.

They are both praised as the answer to training any difficult dog and reviled as an abomination that should be banned outright. It all depends on whom you ask. I suspect that some of the 'experts' most vehemently opposed to them have never seen one in action. I also suspect that their use is rather more widespread than is generally admitted, since there is a natural reluctance to say you have trained your dog using a method that is condemned by some people as being cruel. My own experience with them is limited, but I did once test one out on myself by gripping the collar in my palm and getting Georgina to administer a series of shocks at an increasing distance. I suspect that she enjoyed the experiment rather more than I did. The major effect of the shock was – quite literally – shocking rather than particularly painful. It was certainly not a pleasant sensation, but the discomfort ceased as soon as the transmission stopped, and I would say that it was a lot less unpleasant than being stung with a whippy stick or walloped with the end of a dog lead – both of which many trainers will do to their pupils without a second thought.

How effective an electric collar will be probably depends on the individual dog. I have seen one pointer, that absolutely refused to respond to a turn whistle, brought under control with just a couple of stings from an electric collar. I have also seen a pointer in hot pursuit of a sheep totally ignoring the effect of the collar, possibly because his blood was up to such an extent that he didn't even notice the shocks. Neither may be typical reactions, and I simply don't have enough experience of the use of the collar to write with any real authority on the matter.

My feelings on the subject are that it should be possible, and preferable, to train almost any dog without the need to enlist electronic aids. Man has, after all, been training dogs, more or less successfully, for the past several thousand years. We do perhaps have a tendency today to be less ruthless than some of the trainers of the past, in that we carry on trying to cure faults in our pupils where once only the most promising pups were kept on and those with a tendency to chase sheep or run riot were simply shot and buried.

The one thing that an electric collar can do is to administer punishment at a distance. You can give a command and, if the dog ignores you, you can punish him while he is 'in the act' as it were. There is no doubt that, at times, this is a very handy thing to be able to do. It is also an open invitation to the lazy and the inept to try to skip the basic routine of training and take a shortcut to the finished article. If you do have a problem with stock worrying, or a particularly bone-headed dog that won't respond any other way, then an electric collar may be useful as a cure of last resort. I think though that it would be a great shame if it ever became the standard method of training.

Teaching or Learning?

There are some things that your pupil simply has to be taught. The basic commands to sit, lie down and stay have to be repeated over and over until the dog understands that a particular word, whistle or hand signal means that he should perform a particular action. And then it has to be repeated some more until performing the action has become second nature.

Certain other things can only be learned. Take pointing as an example. You can't teach your dog to point, but he will almost certainly point pretty much instinctively once he gets a noseful of game scent, and then he will learn to seek out similar scents and point them. (I should add that, if we are being pedantic, you actually *can* teach some dogs to point if you spend long enough at it, but a well-bred pointer or setter should do it automatically.)

There are some aspects of training that fall between the two extremes of teaching and learning. Much of the work that pointers and setters do is done using inherited instincts, and it is sometimes possible to overtrain a dog to the extent that what you have taught him overrides the instructions programmed into his genes. If this training stops him from chasing hares then all

You can't teach a dog like this Irish Setter to point – but it is most unlikely that he will not do so quite naturally.

well and good, but if it means that he quarters the ground in an acquired geometric pattern while ignoring the vagaries of the wind then the overall effect of the training may well be counter-productive.

Quartering

Pointers and setters are, first and foremost, hunting dogs. Their job in the shooting field is to find game for the guns, and the emphasis is on the word 'find'. If you know that there are pheasants in a covert, then you don't need a birddog to find them: you need a spaniel or a line of beaters to flush them. Pointers and setters come into their own when you have a few thousand acres of moorland where you believe (or hope) there are a few grouse but need to know exactly where they are before you can shoot them. In order to find them the dog has to get out and hunt. He could just gallop about at random and trust that he would stumble across the odd covey here and there, but it is obviously going to be much more efficient if he has some kind of method to his hunting. Which brings us to the subject of quartering.

Pointers and setters find game by winding the birds' body scent. Depending on scenting conditions (and whole books have been written about scent without anyone being any the wiser about it) they may point game that is fifty or sixty yards ahead of them, or they may run right past birds only ten yards away. Quartering the ground, which is to say running across the wind on one side of the handler, then turning into the wind and going forward a few yards before turning again and making another cast in front of the handler and on to the other side of the beat, is the most efficient way of hunting for game and ensuring that all the ground is covered.

We must be careful for two reasons when we are teaching a dog to quarter. We may, with sufficient dedication, be able to programme our dog to run one hundred and fifty yards out to the side, then turn and go twenty yards forward before turning again and running for three hundred yards in the opposite direction, then going twenty yards forward and three hundred yards back again. It will look very impressive, but it may not be terribly practical. The scent may be so strong that he could find birds fifty yards ahead, or so poor that anything more than ten yards in front will be missed. If our dog religiously sticks to his twenty yards forward on each cast he will either cover nearly three times more ground than necessary, or he will be liable to miss or flush half the birds on the beat. Only the dog can know how good/bad the scent is on a particular day, and if we train him to the extent that he stifles his initiative so that he can follow our orders then we may be making a poor dog out of one that is potentially much better.

We must also take care not to teach the dog to quarter without regard for the wind. Whenever possible a pointer or setter should hunt across the wind, even if it means that he is hunting at an oblique angle to the direction that his handler is taking. I have seen the occasional dog at field trials that was so 'well-trained' that it would hunt a beat at right-angles to the direction that the handler was walking with complete disregard for the way the wind was blowing. It looked good, provided that you ignored the wind direction, but in fact all the dog was doing was running, and not hunting at all.

Gordon Setter. Dogs may be reluctant to quarter if they know there is no game, but a change of ground will usually revive their interest.

So don't be too eager to impose a 'proper' quartering pattern on your dog. If he takes a deeper bite than usual when turning at the end of a cast it could just be that he knows that scent is good and that there are no birds in the next fifty yards. If you make him come back and cross twenty yards in front of you all that you achieve is to waste the dog's effort.

But how do we start him quartering in the first place?

Pointers and setters have been hunting for game by quartering fields and moors for several hundred years, and the instinct to hunt in this manner is, in many cases, built in to them. Left to their own devices many pointer and setters pups will quite naturally range backwards and forwards across the wind. Their quartering will probably be erratic and will certainly be undisciplined, but where the basic instinct exists the task of the trainer is not so much to teach the dog to quarter as to refine that instinct so that the dog quarters to a satisfactory pattern. In other cases quartering may have to be taught virtually from scratch, but even where a young dog initially seems to have no instinct for ground treatment it is quite possible that, after a few lessons, he will suddenly discover some natural talent that was previously hidden.

Take your pup out into an open area and allow him to run free while you are walking slowly into the wind, and see how he reacts. If he shows a tendency to range from side to side across the wind then he probably has the rudiments of quartering fixed in his brain already. Even if he doesn't react in this way there is no cause for despair. Some dogs display hunting and pointing instincts almost from the time they are old enough to walk, while others may be well on the way to adulthood before their natural ability seems to kick in. The very fact of encouraging him to range in an appropriate manner may be enough to awaken those latent instincts.

There are several ways of training your dog to quarter, and all of them involve getting him actually ranging from side to side. At the most basic you can walk – or run if you are sufficiently athletic – from side to side, across the face of the wind, with the dog on his lead beside you. As you reach the limit of each cast – and I would advise keeping these casts quite short – you give the turn signal on your whistle and bring the dog round, *turning into the wind*, and then start off on your next cast. When you reach the end of this cast you give the turn signal again and once again turn into the wind and start back across your beat.

After the first lessons on a normal lead you can progress to running the dog on a check cord. This has the advantage of letting the dog actually run instead of walking, or at best trotting, on a short lead. The procedure is the same: start the dog off across the wind in one direction, then, as he is getting to the end of his line, give the turn signal. If he turns of his own accord: great. If he doesn't, give a jerk on the line to turn him and bring him onto the opposite tack.

Take care not to let him bore forward at this stage. Later on, when he is experienced at running on the hill and finding game, a good dog will use his own judgement to decide how big a forward cast he can make without missing birds. In these early lessons though you are trying to accustom him to hunting under your control, and to looking to you for instructions rather than running on instinct alone.

This is also a good time to start getting the dog accustomed to the idea of working to hand signals. Signalling him to go left or right is done by extending your arm in the appropriate direction almost as if sending him on by the force of the gesture. If you give a hand signal as you set him off, and then another as he crosses in front of you on each cast he should soon come to associate the gesture with the action of running in a particular direction. Initially you are not looking for a young dog to obey a hand signal, but rather to get used to the idea that when he sees that particular movement of your arm he should run in the direction of the movement.

Once the dog is starting to turn on your whistle signal rather than having to be brought round with a tug on the check cord you can begin to extend his range. If you are fit enough you can do this initially by running from side to side with him – or rather behind him, because you are certainly not going to be able to keep up – and bringing him round after a somewhat wider cast. The time to start running to your right, for example, is as soon as the dog starts in that direction from his left-hand cast. If you wait until he has gone past you he will be at the end of his check cord almost before you get into your stride. You can achieve a similar effect by lengthening the check cord, but it is quite difficult to manage very long lines unless you are training your dog on short-cropped grass. If you try to work him on two hundred yards of line on heather moorland or anywhere with bushes or scrub all that will happen is that you, he and the cord will end up in an enormous fankle.

As you progress you can let the end of the line go and allow the dog a certain amount more freedom. Give him a few extra yards to range out on the flank before turning him with the whistle and bringing him back across the front of your beat. If he turns to command all well and good. If he doesn't, ignores your whistle and carries on until he is ready to turn himself, then try and catch the check cord when he eventually crosses in front of you again and then bring him round with a jerk on the cord at the end of his next beat, having, of course, given the turn signal on your whistle. The fact that he is trailing a length of cord behind him makes it a lot easier to catch him than if he were running free, when the only way to bring him back under control is to physically get hold of him. If you can get your hand or your foot onto the check cord you can let him run on a few yards and then give him his turn signal – *and enforce it.* This is much better than simply catching him up and putting him back on his lead because you should be able to continue on a positive rather than a negative note.

Always try to get the dog to turn into the wind, rather than back casting. Initially, when he is running on his check cord, this is relatively easy because you can take a few steps forward as he is casting out so that when you bring him round you will be tugging him into the wind. Some dogs will tend to turn in the same direction – i.e. to their right, or their left, – at the end of each cast, thus casting forward on one side and backwards on the other. This is an inefficient way of hunting because some ground is always covered twice while other bits are missed, but it is not the end of the world in a working dog. If he is coming along reasonably well in other respects, and you are training him for shooting, a tendency to back cast may not be a problem. If your aim is to compete in field trials with the dog though it is important to try and get him turning into the wind on every cast, because a dog that back casts regularly is always going to be at a disadvantage in the eyes of the judges.

Some pointers and setters can be taught – perhaps encouraged would be a better word – to quarter without recourse to check cords. Face into the wind and set your pup off running to one side. Once he is away, turn and walk in the opposite direction and call or whistle him to come to you. When he arrives encourage him to carry on across the wind, then take a few steps forward, turn away from him again and whistle or call him back. Initially keep the distance that he goes out from you short, and also keep the lesson short, stopping while he is still enjoying the game.

It may help if you can start this off in a convenient field with a good fence on either side so that there is a natural barrier if he decides to take himself too far off to the sides, but it is still important that your direction of travel is into the wind. You are trying to get him into the habit of using the wind to hunt. If you ignore the direction of the wind there is a danger that you will end up teaching him to run in a pretty pattern regardless of the wind and a dog that ignores the wind when he is hunting is next to useless.

This free running method of training the dog to quarter is obviously best if you have a dog that is fairly responsive and already accustomed to coming to you when he is called. You may prefer to start off training him using a check cord and then progress to this when he has grasped the basic idea of quartering.

Using a check cord to ensure that this young Irish Setter holds his point until the gun is in position.

Using a hand signal to emphasise the drop command, though in this case the dog is concentrating on the grouse and will not have seen the signal.

Casting off at a field trial – pointers and setters should always work across the wind to find their quarry.

These lessons are best taught initially in the absence of game. This may be a problem, depending on what sort of ground you have available for training your dog. You may have a local park or sports field that has the space you require as well as being pretty well guaranteed not to hold any game, but some dogs are simply not interested in 'hunting' when their eyes and, more importantly, their noses tell them that there is nothing whatsoever to hunt.

When you first begin training, provided that the dog has not already started to learn to hunt of his own accord, it shouldn't be too difficult to get him running, even if you are on the local football pitch. If, after a few lessons, he begins to be reluctant to quarter, you may be able to re-kindle his interest by taking him onto fresh ground. If you have a number of fields available for training then switching around regularly will help to keep him keen and interested.

At this stage the objective of your training should be to get the pup to the point where he will run across the wind, turn into the wind at the end of each cast and be reasonably responsive to your commands, particularly to your turn whistle. It is neither desirable nor necessary to expect him to be running an apparently perfect pattern in a bare field, because only when he has started to get some experience of game, and of the capabilities of his nose, will he be able to quarter in an efficient manner. Remember that only the dog can tell what the scent is like at any one moment. What looks right to you may not be right at all.

There is a limit to how far you can take your quartering training on a bare field or a town park. Once the principle appears to be taken on board you can start to make things more interesting for both yourself and your pupil by getting out onto ground where there is at least

the possibility of him coming across something to point when he is quartering. Ideally, you would have regular access to heather moorland, preferably with some ground where there was grouse and somewhere you could train your dog in the reasonable expectation that there would not be any game to distract him. For some fortunate individuals – moorland keepers, grouse moor owners and the like – this may well be the case, but most of us will have to make the best of what is available.

Always remember that, once your dog starts working properly he will have to adjust his quartering pattern to suit the prevailing conditions, and he will only be able to do that by learning from experience. Precise, geometric patterns of quartering may look very impressive, whether drawn out on paper or actually described on the hill, but they are only a means to an end: not an end in themselves. The job of a pointer or setter is to find game and in the shooting field a dog that quarters erratically but finds birds is of far more use than one that quarters immaculately but misses them. That said, if all other things are equal, a dog which quarters his ground properly will always be more efficient than one that bores, back casts and wanders about aimlessly.

Introduction to Game

Once your pup starts to come into contact with game, be it grouse, partridge, pheasant, woodcock, snipe or some other game bird, you have a number of other lessons to impart. He has to be encouraged to remain steady on point, to rode in and flush the birds when you tell him, and to drop, or at the least, not to give chase, when the birds take to the wing. There is not a cut-off point between quartering and game handling, when one phase of training ends and the other begins. As you start to get your dog out onto more 'gamey' ground, so it is likely that he will find and point birds. When he does, the quartering lesson becomes a game-handling lesson.

Bringing a young Pointer in behind the pointing dog to give him a first scent of game.

Don't be tempted to rush this introduction to game because you 'want to see if he will point'. If he is a well-bred pointer or setter, particularly one from working stock, it is extremely unlikely that he will not point game. There are several hundred years of breeding in his genes compelling him to do just that. An early introduction to game will tell you nothing useful whatsoever. If he does point: well, so what? He's a pointer (or a setter) and that is what he's bred to do. If a youngster fails to point, flushes birds or doesn't seem too interested in them: well, again: so what? The best dog I have ever owned showed no interest whatsoever in grouse until he was about eighteen months old, and at the time we were living right in the middle of a grouse moor, so he saw, or scented grouse nearly every day and mostly simply ignored them. Then, quite suddenly, his instincts kicked in and he became as steady and reliable a pointer as any I have ever seen.

I have owned other dogs that were pointing flies on the wall or butterflies in the garden almost before they could walk. The instinct to point is inbred, and it is a very rare pointer or setter indeed that won't stop and point when he has a good noseful of game scent. Don't worry about it: get on with your training programme and trust that he will know what to do, quite instinctively, when he suddenly finds himself downwind of a grouse, a partridge or a pheasant.

What we want him to do when that happens is threefold. One, he needs to stay steady on point until we tell him to do something else. Two, we want him to rode in on the scent and flush the birds. And three we want him *not* to roar off in pursuit. One and two are generally easy because pointing and then roding in is doing what his natural instincts are urging him to do. Three is something else. He's found this wonderful smell, pointed it, crept in until he is right up close to the source, and suddenly the owner of the smell has erupted out of the heather or grass in front of him and fluttered off just begging to be chased. This is the moment when we discover just how well those lessons on dropping to a whistle have been ingrained.

If you have been running your pup on a check cord there is a good chance that you will be able to get hold of the end of the line before you go up to where he is pointing. If so you will be able to take your time getting up to him and gently hold him back if he shows signs of creeping forward before you are ready. Even if he is running free of a line you may still be able to slip a lead or a check cord over his head before encouraging him to go on and flush his birds. Once you and the dog are connected by opposite ends of a piece of string you can be quite confident of getting him to drop to flush and not to chase.

Go right up to him, tell him what a good dog he is and keep him waiting for a few seconds more before you snap your fingers, or tell him to 'Get on' or 'Get him out' or whatever command takes your fancy. If he shows signs of wanting to charge in and flush his birds steady him up: if he is reluctant to move then encourage him gently forward. When the birds finally rise, give the drop command and, if you have to, gently push him down to the ground. And then tell him what a good boy he is, and let him go forward and 'clear his ground' or hunt out the bit of cover from which the birds rose.

Then it is just a matter of repeating the procedure whenever he finds game, always trying to ensure that he drops when the birds flush, or at the least, stays where he is and doesn't give chase. It is sometimes said that the reason pointers and setters are required to drop to flush is so that they will not be in the line of fire from the guns. This is patently not true. No gun should ever be fired directly over the top of a dog for a start. The guns should be alongside and preferably a little bit ahead of where the dog is pointing. And even if the guns were shooting from behind the dog, the idea that anyone should fire a shot so close to the dog that he had to lie down in order to be out of the path of the pellets is simply ludicrous.

There are though a couple of very good reasons for insisting on your dogs dropping to wing and to shot. Dropping, or lying down when he sees a bird get up or hears a shot fired gives the

Field trial dogs must remain steady no matter what the temptation.

dog something definite to do on these occasions, and having done it he is not in a position from which he can suddenly take off running. Just not going forward when birds flush is rather nebulous in comparison, and it is not something you can practise during your training sessions. The drop, on the other hand, is something that you should have been teaching and practising with your pup right from the start of his training, and it is something that you can go on practising for as long as you feel he needs the discipline.

Once having dropped there is a definite break in the action from the dog's point of view. He may know very well that there are more birds ahead of him, but as long as he is down on the ground there is less temptation for him to creep on and start working out the ones that didn't rise in the first flush. He is down in the heather, or the stubble, and he should be waiting for your specific command before he does anything else. Primarily and historically, he is waiting to give the guns time to reload. In the days of muzzle-loaders this could have meant a couple of minutes or more, depending on how keen and how efficient the guns were at the reloading procedure: today most guns can get a couple of cartridges into the breech in a matter of seconds – particularly if they think there is the prospect of another shot.

If you only have one dog then you may have to chance to luck in getting him onto game for the first few times. If you already have an experienced working birddog – or can enlist the help of someone else who does – then you may be able to get the older dog to find game for you, then bring your pupil in behind the point to get his first experience of game scent.

Backing: though it is likely that the second Pointer has the scent of the covey as well as the pointing dog.

The theory is quite simple. You, or your friend, works the experienced dog until it comes on point. Then you bring your young dog in behind the pointing dog so that he is getting the same scent carried on the breeze that has caused the other dog to stop and point. If all goes to plan your pup should get a good noseful of scent and stiffen up into a point himself. If all goes to plan.

Have we considered backing yet? Backing is the term used to describe the, generally instinctive, action of a pointer or setter whereby, when it sees another dog pointing, it points *at the pointing dog*. Note that phrase carefully. A backing dog is 'backing' (or pointing at) the dog that is already on point. It is *not* pointing the game that the first dog is pointing. It is not 'giving the guns a cross-reference on the position of the birds', nor is it 'confirming that there is game present' as I have heard claimed on occasion. It is pointing the pointing dog, or, in the correct parlance, it is 'backing' him.

Pointing is induced by scent: backing by sight. Some pointers and setters will back sheep, or tree stumps or white rocks, or anything that looks to them like another dog on point. Some, in complete contrast, will go to any lengths to subdue their natural instinct to back, even carefully avoiding looking at another dog on point. The important thing to remember though is that the very sight of another dog on point tends to induce an instinctive reaction in pointers and setters, and that reaction is to freeze, just as if they were on point, and back the pointing dog.

This is, by and large, a good thing. If you are ever working a brace of dogs (i.e. running two dogs simultaneously) then, if one finds birds it is an excellent idea for the other one to stop hunting while you get your guns into position and work out the point. You don't want him running on and flushing those birds, or rushing up to the pointing dog and inducing a fit of jealously that will probably also result in a flush. This is not a modern concept: exactly the same thing applied a hundred or two hundred years ago. And since the instinct to back another dog is clearly useful in a pointer or setter, it was one of the things that the old breeders kept in mind when they were selecting their stock. So it is quite likely that your dog will instinctively stiffen up and back the experienced dog as soon as he sees it on point.

Now you have something of a dilemma. Backing another dog, and staying steady in the backing position is a good thing in a working or a trialling dog. You do not want to teach your pup that the thing to do when he sees another dog on point is to march right on up to it. If he is backing you want to encourage him and steady him so that he learns that backing is the correct thing to do when another dog has found birds. Be very wary of giving him the impression that backing is less important than getting up to where the birds are hiding. I would suggest that, if your pup backs the other dog, you encourage him to stay steady and let the other handler flush the birds: then drop your dog when he sees them taking wing. If he is a natural backer you should be encouraging it: not moving him on against his instincts.

If, on the other hand, he is quite happy to trot along and in behind the pointing dog until he gets the scent himself and also starts to point, then taking a young dog in behind an older dog can be a useful way of introducing him to game under conditions in which you are in control. If the lie of the ground is favourable you may be able, by taking a roundabout route, to get your pupil in close to the pointing dog before he can actually see it. If you can get within scenting range of the birds the natural instinct to point should override the compulsion to back.

Two Pointers provide a classic example of backing during a grouse count.

One thing you should not do is to allow your dog to go past the pointing dog and, in effect, steal his point. This is bad for both pupil and experienced dog because it teaches the youngster that it is acceptable to go past another dog on point, and it is liable to make the older dog jealous. Next time he hears, sees or senses another dog coming in behind or alongside him he may just decide to go and flush 'his' birds before the other dog takes over. It is possible to ruin a good dog very easily in just a few thoughtless moments.

When your dog first starts hunting he is liable to point pretty nearly everything. Pipits and larks have a sufficiently interesting scent to bring most birddogs onto point, and I once had a dog that produced a remarkably staunch point on a frog. This presents the trainer with something of a dilemma. Should you praise the dog for pointing and holding his point – assuming that he has – or should you tell him off for pointing pipits?

In the early stages of training it is as well to encourage any pointing activity. After all: until the lark, pipit or whatever actually flushes you won't know what he was pointing anyway. The odds are that the more experience he gets, and the more exposure to proper game bird scent, the less he will be inclined to point pipits and the like. Once you start shooting over them most dogs quickly come to understand what it is they are supposed to be hunting.

Hares and Rabbits

There are few things more tempting to a dog than the sight of a rabbit or a hare, bouncing along ahead of him and positively inviting him to come and play. Left to their own devices, practically any dog, from a Chihuahua to a Great Dane, will chase rabbits and hares. Pointers and setters are no exception. There is an additional complication in the case of pointing dogs in that, not only do we not want them to chase fur, but we in general don't want them to point it either.

If you are planning to use your pointer or setter for rough shooting then I suppose it is possible that you may *want* him to point rabbits and hares as well as game birds. The chances are he will point them anyway without any encouragement. If though, you are going to be working him on grouse or partridge, and particularly if you plan to compete in field trials, pointing rabbits is definitely not something you want to see. Hares, as far as trials are concerned, are something of an enigma. If your dog points a hare he can be credited with the find, but if he simply ignores hares he will not be punished for missing them.

In the early stages of training it is certainly not a good idea to punish a dog for pointing fur for fear you discourage him from pointing altogether. As he gets more experience, particularly if he is being shot over regularly, he will probably learn that rabbits (and hares, if such is the case) are not wanted. You can help the process along by scolding him when he produces fur and praising him when he finds feathered game, and he will also get the message as he sees what game is shot and what is ignored. I need hardly say that, if you don't want him to point rabbits, then never allow anyone to shoot rabbits over him. And the same goes for hares.

Pointing the odd rabbit or hare during a shoot day may not seem such a big problem, and it may not be a problem provided that it is only 'the odd rabbit or hare'. Trouble starts when you are working him on the sort of moor that has a big population of either. Then you may find your dog on point every few moments, and time after time you will be leading the guns in to position only to see a rabbit or hare scuttle away. With some dogs you can tell when he is pointing a rabbit or a hare because he will have his ears up and a slightly guilty look. Even so, unless you were very, very sure about your dog it would be a brave handler who told the guns 'It's just a rabbit,' and marched off alone to pick up the dog and set him quartering again, because the chances are that when you got to the dog you would flush the biggest covey of grouse you would see all day. This would be even less popular than taking the guns in to a point on a rabbit.

The answer to most of the problems of pointing the wrong things, be they hares, rabbits, pipits, larks (or even frogs!) is to get the dog out working. Most dogs will learn, sooner or later, what gets shot and what is left to fly or run away unscathed. Once that is established in their minds there is a very good chance that they will stop pointing the things you don't want pointed and concentrate on the grouse, partridges, pheasants, or whatever it is you may be hunting.

Chasing and Running In

For most handlers the problem associated with hares and rabbits is not so much whether the dog will point them, or not, but how to stop him from chasing them.

We should perhaps begin by defining the difference between 'chasing' and 'running in', since they are not quite the same things. Running in is taking off when a bird is shot; usually with the intention of making a retrieve. This is a fault of course, but a less serious one than giving chase indiscriminately, where the dog simply sets off in hot pursuit of birds or ground game, and in some cases sheep and deer. Giving chase when game is in sight is, once again, simply a dog obeying his natural instincts, so once again, it is your job as his trainer to teach him that where giving chase is concerned he must learn to suppress those instincts.

In theory this is quite a simple procedure. You take your pup out to a place where you can expect him to find hares or rabbits or game birds and you set him off to work. Then, when he finds a hare or a rabbit or a pheasant, flushes it and starts to chase you blow your drop whistle and he immediately abandons the chase and drops. You praise him for the good dog that he is and maybe repeat the dose. He gets the idea and thereafter he drops to fur and to wing. What could be easier than that?

Except that we should consider the possibility that he won't abandon his chase and drop when he hears your whistle. Maybe he will be so excited by the chase that he will either fail to hear the whistle or simply decide to ignore it. If so, sterner measures are required.

Beware of punishing your dog when he eventually comes back to you at the end of the chase. There is the obvious danger that he will associate the punishment with coming back to you rather than with giving chase, and the consequence is likely to be that he becomes reluctant to come to you for fear of further punishment. Ideally, you would train him to drop to flying birds or running animals by repetition and enforcement of the drop command whenever game flies or runs off in front of him. When training pointers and setters this is sometimes easier to achieve than when working with flushing dogs such as spaniels because you generally have the chance to get right up to the dog as he points game, and slip a lead or a check cord around his neck if you so choose.

Once he is on his check lead, either because he was running on it anyway, or because you popped it round his neck while he was on point, it is relatively simple to ensure that your commands are obeyed. If he doesn't drop when you order him down you can jerk him back sharply as you give the command for the second time. Depending on how bone-headed your particular pupil is, it should not take too many repetitions before the penny drops and the dog starts to do the same. Then all you have to do is to reinforce the behaviour by repeating the lesson until it becomes automatic. This doesn't mean getting him to drop countless times during a single training session, but rather that you repeat the lesson once or twice per session over several weeks if that is practical.

Chasing farm stock is obviously a far more serious problem than running in or chasing game. Some dogs never show the slightest interest in sheep or deer, nor any inclination to chase them: others, unfortunately, can be hell-bent on chasing. If they are, then the fault must be eradicated, or the dog is effectively useless as a working dog.

It is very important that the dog does not run in: if this Pointer had not been quite steady he could easily have been in the line of fire.

Sheep chasing seems to be an inherited instinct and one that can even get worse from generation to generation. If you are unfortunate enough to own a truly dedicated sheep chaser there is probably no cure other than keeping the dog on a lead, away from all farm stock, and only working him on ground where there are no sheep. This particular problem may even equate with a bullet and a burial in the worst cases. There are several possible 'cures' for sheep chasers, but none that guarantee success. One of the problems with this particular fault is that you can never be sure that it has been totally eradicated. Your dog may work right through the middle of sheep for day after day without giving them a glance, then suddenly decide to chase one for no apparent reason.

If you know a friendly farmer you may be able to try the traditional 'cure' of penning the dog in with a ewe with a lamb at foot, or with a ram, and letting the sheep give the dog a few dunts with its head or horns. This can prove a very salutary experience for the dog and the temptation to chase is obviously less if the dog has been persuaded that catching up with the sheep is likely to result in bruised ribs for the chaser. Keep a close watch on proceedings if you do try this. I heard of a case where a lurcher was supposedly being 'cured' of sheep chasing. The owner dumped him in a stall with a ram, closed the door and went for a cup of tea. By the time he came back, the dog was dead.

Even if you can find a sufficiently aggressive sheep and friendly farmer to try this cure the results are not guaranteed. There is a world of difference between being locked in a confined space with an angry tup, and being out on the hill with a bunch of ewes and lambs fleeing in panic before you, and your dog will almost certainly appreciate the difference.

Chasing is never easy to cure if it once becomes ingrained. In an ideal world our young dogs would be so well disciplined on their drop whistle that they would invariably obey it every time the temptation to chase arose. Then, by repetition, they would get into the habit of dropping when a hare leapt up or a bird flushed. Sadly, we do not live in an ideal world, and it is not impossible that your pup will have a tendency to give chase when a hare pops up under his nose and may not drop when you give a blast on your Thunderer. Now is the time we must hope you have him on his check cord and can bring him up sharply and then explain the error of his ways. If he is running free and gets away to enjoy a good, long gallop, then you had better make sure that he is on a check cord next time.

The task of teaching a dog not to give chase is tackled in exactly the same way as getting him to sit or to turn on a whistle. You give the command, see that he does what he is supposed to do, and keep repeating the lesson until he obeys automatically. The difference is that his attention is probably on you, and he may have nothing better to do than to sit when you give the command. If a rabbit has just bolted right in front of him he quite definitely has something other than you on his mind, and can think of far more interesting ways of spending the next few seconds than parking his backside on the ground in response to a peep on your whistle. You just have to persevere.

Running in to shot or to the fall of game is something that is liable to start once you begin shooting over your dog. A lady owner once brought a beautifully trained German Pointer to a shoot in the north of Scotland, hoping to shoot some grouse over him during her week's stay. I happened to overhear her conversation with the estate owner.

'He's never been worked on grouse,' she said, 'But he's very steady, and he doesn't run in.' Her host's reply was immediate.

'He will by the end of the week.'

And he did.

It is hardly surprising, after running several miles over the heather in order to find birds and point them that, when he suddenly sees a bird or two dropping into the heather a few yards in front of him, he decides to go and investigate. If he is one of those pointers or setters with an affinity for retrieving he may well pick one of them up and bring it back to you. Actually getting hold of the quarry is the natural conclusion to a successful hunt as far as any dog is concerned. He's found the birds; someone has shot one; he's gone and collected it and brought it back to the boss. In the early days of his shooting career the sight of a bird falling will be an entirely novel experience, and it is up to you to ensure that he learns to react to that experience by dropping, or at least by staying where he is rather than running in.

The most important time in any dog's shooting life is his first shooting season, and particularly the first few days of that season. There is all the excitement associated with shooting as opposed to training sessions: you will be keyed up as will the guns, the other dogs, the keeper and the host, and that excitement will transfer to your dog. Now is the time to ensure that you are fully focussed on keeping your dog right. Never mind marking down shot birds or watching to see where the covey lands: keep all your attention on your dog and make sure that he drops to the flush and stays dropped until you tell him to get up again. And next time he has a point, do it again, and then again and again.

More dogs are spoilt during their first few days out shooting rather than at any other time. If you can keep on top of your dog and maintain discipline in these first few, vital days in the field then you may never have any problem with him. If you lose control now you may never be able to get it back again.

Although in some senses we never really 'finish' training our dogs, once we start taking them shooting there is a subtle difference in what goes on. When we are training a dog we are generally teaching him to act in certain ways. Once he starts working regularly he will begin to learn about his craft. Note the difference of emphasis between 'teaching' and 'learning'. We still have to guide our pupil and try to keep him on the straight and narrow, but from now on he will be learning rather than being taught. This is particularly true of pointers and setters who are working well away from their handlers.

If you are training a Labrador you have far more opportunity to engineer situations and to keep him away from potential problems during these early days in the field. You can select your retrieves: keep him closely at heel during drives: only send him for birds that you are sure are dead and generally keep him away from awkward situations. With a pointer or setter, quartering the open hill several hundred yards away from you, it is far more difficult to keep a young dog out of trouble. Even so, we should do our best, and one of the things we will consider in the next chapter is how best to introduce our tyro to his life's work.

Chapter 7
Working Pointers and Setters

It is most important that a young dog should have its first bird killed to it in a correct manner, and it is always best that a good shot, who is standing well out on a flank from a young dog's point, should fire one shot only, and kill one bird stone dead in front of the dog. The dog scarcely hears the shot because his attention is on the birds, and after being made to drop at the fall of the birds, he is led gently to the dead bird and allowed to nose it. The young dog is now 'made'....
Dugald Macintyre – writing in *Shooting By Moor, Field and Shore* The Lonsdale Library, 1929

The advice reprinted above is as relevant today as it was when Dugald Macintyre originally penned it three-quarters of a century ago. The most important days in a young dog's life are those when he first goes to the shooting field. Get everything just right to begin with and the dog may be 'made' for life. Sadly the converse is also true. Lose control of your dog in those first few vital hours and days and you may never get it back again. Months and months of patient work can be ruined in minutes.

'...a good shot should fire one shot only and kill one bird stone dead in front of the dog.'

Dugald Macintyre's words are a counsel of perfection. It would be wonderful if we were able to arrange our dog's first 'real' point in such a way that a gun standing on the flank would 'fire one shot only and kill one bird stone dead in front of the dog'. We can try of course, but what if the gun misses with the first shot? Should he fire a second? And what if he misses with that one too? Or only wounds the bird instead of killing it stone dead? Events in the shooting field have a habit of not working out exactly as planned – and this is most often the case when we have tried particularly hard to produce a certain outcome. Ask anyone who has changed pegs at a drive in order to ensure that a guest gets the best of the shooting – a move that is absolutely guaranteed to give the guest a blank drive while every pheasant in the covert streams over the peg he had originally drawn.

Shooting over dogs is even less susceptible to forward planning than driven shooting. Coveys are not found where they were expected, or are found where they were not. Grouse, that should sit tightly on a hot August day, may decide to run or to raise their heads and jump precipitously despite the weather. Scent may be excellent or awful: birds may rise singly or all in a bunch: the wind may drop, or rise, or change direction altogether. And however good a shot a gun may be, nobody can guarantee to kill a bird stone dead with a single shot.

So whatever I or any other writer may advise about introducing a young dog to shooting, or working dogs in general, it is important to approach the matter with an open mind, the ability to think on your feet, and a willingness to adapt your grand plan to whatever the day may bring. Three things to bear in mind are:

1 Try to keep things as simple as possible
2 Make certain the guns know what you are trying to do
3 Quit while you're ahead.

Riven with hags and gullies, a moor like this is not the ideal place to introduce a young dog to the shooting field.

Let us look at those things in a little more detail. Keeping things simple means making sure that you start your young dog off working into the wind, and preferably on a nice, open piece of moor where you can see what he is doing, rather than somewhere riven with gullies and peat hags where the wind will twist and swirl and your dog will be out of sight most of the time. It also helps if you are reasonably confident of finding a grouse or a covey before your dog has had time to become exhausted or bored.

Keeping the guns 'on message' can be equally important. Let them know before you set your dog off for the first time that he is an inexperienced youngster and that you don't want them loosing off shots at stray birds while he is running, nor encouraging their spaniels to go snuffling about under his nose when he is on point. (You wouldn't want either of those things to happen anyway, but it is especially important to avoid them when you are just starting out with a new dog.) When he does point take the guns in quietly and steadily and keep them well off to the side of the dog. You don't want them rushing up to the point in great excitement and perhaps starting the dog roding in before you are ready, nor do you want someone to fire a shot right next to the dog's ear. Get the guns on your side from the start. And when, hopefully, you have had a couple of points and your dog has behaved impeccably, *stop*. Pick him up, put him on the lead, and let the other dogs do the work for the rest of the day. In other words, quit while you're ahead.

If the opportunity arises and you can arrange to go grouse counting before the season proper opens on the Twelfth you will have the chance to break your young dog in rather more gently than if you start him off directly under fire. The grouse count can be a valuable service to a gamekeeper or shoot manager keen to get a good idea of his prospects in advance of the season, and it is an absolutely invaluable way for the

Grouse counting is ideal for introducing young dogs to game and for reminding older dogs of their manners.

dog trainer to get his team out onto the heather before shooting starts. All dogs, and their handlers, need to get fit ready for the shooting season, and there is no better way of getting ready for the hill than spending a few days actually working your dogs on the heather.

You have the chance to remind the older dogs of their manners: of the need to hold their points, to drop when birds flush, to refrain from running in or chasing hares and the like. The young dogs can get their first introduction to grouse and heather without the distraction of guns firing and birds dropping, and without the pressure that comes from having to show sport for a team of guns. You can stop for a rest, or a break to calm the dogs down whenever it suits you, and there is generally no obligation to put in a full day's work if your dogs are not yet fit.

Remember though, that for the young, inexperienced dog getting an introduction to the hill, much the same rules apply to grouse counting as they do to shooting. You don't have any guns to worry about, but you should still try to ensure that your young dog is given nice, simple, into the wind work to begin with, and not run on and on until he is tired and starts making mistakes through a loss of concentration.

Incidentally, it is also important to remember that the reason you are there, as far as the keeper is concerned, is to conduct a grouse count. He is not going to be delighted if, at the end of the day, you can tell him in great detail how well your dog worked but are a little vague about the number of grouse you have seen. If the keeper accompanies you then the problem does not arise, but if you are out on your own it is as well to take a pencil and a little notebook and keep a proper record of what birds you find. Note how many coveys and how many barren pairs or singles you see and roughly where they were. Count the number of grouse in each covey and note whether they were well grown and strong on the wing, a little bit immature, or just cheepers. Watch where the birds alight after you have flushed them and take care not to double count. Try not to flush birds more than once: if you have seen a covey pitch in to a particular spot it is best to keep the dogs away from there if it is practical.

In that brief look at how you might best introduce your young dog to the shooting field we have touched on the three things that you must be concerned with whenever you are working your dogs. You must:

1 Handle your dog,
2 Control your guns, and
3 Generally organise the shooting day.

That you need to handle the dog is obvious. Control of the guns may not seem to be your direct responsibility though, and surely it is the job of the keeper, the host or the shoot manager to organise the shooting day? Yes, it is: up to a point, but if you are to get the best from your dogs, and thus give the best possible day to the guns, then it is quite likely that you will have to do a certain amount of tactful organising of the guns and of the day in general.

Organising the Day

We are going to assume that the 'day' in question takes place on a grouse moor in August. You could equally well be working your dogs on partridge coveys among the stubbles and roots of early autumn, or hunting for snipe and woodcock on an Irish bog at the beginning of winter, but whatever the season and the situation the same rules apply.

When a party of guns set out to shoot over pointers or setters the responsibility on the dogs and their handler is far greater than that resting on a picker-up or a member of the beating team on a driven shoot. In the latter cases it won't make too much difference in the great scheme of things if your dog doesn't cover himself with glory. You are just one of a team, and if he doesn't flush a particular pheasant or collect a runner when he is sent to retrieve there is every chance that one of the other dogs will do it in his stead. If he misbehaves badly you can put a lead round his neck and simply give up and go home or carry on with him firmly under control by your side. The team may be one beater short, but it probably won't make any discernible difference to the bag at the end of the day.

Now consider the role of the dogs when the guns are shooting over pointers and setters. Their job is to find birds for the guns. If they don't, then the guns will have no shooting. Full stop. The whole success or lack of success of the day rests on your shoulders and, more pertinently, on the shoulders of your dogs. Do a good job and – provided there are some grouse – your guns will have a good day. Make a mess of things and….

But you are not going to make a mess of things, and nor are your dogs. And one way to ensure that things do go according to plan is to ensure that everyone knows what they are doing, right from the start.

I am not suggesting that you have to turn up with your team of dogs and then start telling the Head Keeper, with his fifty years of experience on the grouse moors, how he should run the shoot. When you start and when you finish, which beat you are working, the bag limit, if there is one, and any local rules such as whether snipe or blackgame are to be shot are not really your concern, though you may have some thoughts about how long a day your dogs can manage. Some other points though are very much your business, and it is as well to make sure that everyone knows exactly what they are going to be doing before you make a start.

Get everyone together: the guns, the keeper, the picker-up if there is one and any incidental bodies such as husbands, wives, girlfriends, boyfriends or children. Get the usual niceties out of the way and then have a little chat about what you will all be doing once the first dog is cast off. Discreetly check with the keeper, or whoever is organising the day, whether they are knowledgeable about and experienced in shooting over pointers and setters. If they know the rules already they may prefer to be the one who explains things to the rest of the party. Just make sure in advance that you are both working to the same script. You do not want the keeper to start off, for example, by telling the guns they will be walking in line only for you to have to interrupt and tell them that they won't.

The first thing to establish is how much experience, if any, the guns have of shooting over pointers. It may be that you are going out with two guns who have been shooting over dogs for the last thirty years and know more about the game than you do. Even so, it is still advisable to run through the rules with them. If your guns are new to the game then it is far easier to tell them what they should be doing now, while you have their full attention, than to try doing it when there is a dog on point, people scattered all over the hill, grouse getting up wild and a couple of spaniels racketing about in front of the pointing dog. So what do you need to tell them?

The first thing to get established in everyone's mind is that they are shooting *over dogs*. They are not walking up grouse (or partridge, or snipe, or woodcock, or whatever). There is a common misconception that shooting over dogs involves a team of guns walking in line across the hill with the dog working away in front of them. The occasional gun thinks he should be able to wander along with his own dog hunting just in front of him for any birds the pointers have missed, while your dog works away ahead of the line. This is not only wrong, it is downright dangerous, and absolute anathema to decent pointer and setter work. Do not allow it to happen under any circumstances.

There is nothing wrong with shooting grouse by walking in line with spaniels or Labradors hunting in front of you – provided that you are not trying to shoot over pointers at the same time. A line of guns spread across the hill can cover a front of several hundred yards. It is a natural tendency among many pointers and setters to work out to and then beyond the end gun

Have a chat with the guns at the start of the day to make sure you all know what you are doing. Ben Ferny, Peter Ord, Frank Yorke and John Clunas were the guns at the Balmoral International Match.

94   *Walking up grouse in line is emphatically not the same thing as shooting them over dogs.*

on either flank. If the walking guns are reasonably fit, or over-keen, they will tend to push your dogs not only wider, but also further and further forward as the dog tries to stay ahead of the guns. Birds can then be missed by the pointer and possibly walked up by the guns and their own dogs. Picture the situation.

Your dog is quartering fifty or sixty yards ahead of the line of guns. A covey of grouse springs out of the heather and splits to either side of the line. Two, three, perhaps four of the walking guns see the chance of a shot at those birds skimming low across the heather. Their full concentration is on those speeding brown shapes, they are swinging their guns into their shoulders as fast as they can before the grouse are out of range – and your dog is right in the line of fire. This is not one of those hypothetical situations by which it is just possible that, given an unlikely combination of circumstances and some really bad luck a dog might just get stung with a stray pellet. There is a very real chance of your dogs being killed or seriously injured.

A friend of mine was working her Irish Setter for a shooting party a few years ago – not actually in front of a line of guns, but on a downwind beat so that the dog was working back towards the guns. A grouse jumped from under their feet; one of the party was carrying a loaded gun and took a snap shot, and my friend was left with a blind Irish Setter. You can only imagine just how distressing this was for the gun who fired the shot and for the owner of the dog, let alone the poor setter himself. There is not much future for a blind working setter.

So no walking in line when you are shooting over pointers and setters. Keep everyone together a few yards behind you. It is a far more civilised way to spend the day than marching in line abreast spread out over a quarter of a mile of hill. The party can talk – quietly it is hoped – among themselves. Guns can be left empty until a dog points. If someone wants to stop for a rest, or a smoke, or a drink then you can call in the dog and everyone can have a break for ten minutes. There is no pressure to cover miles and miles of ground: no need to exhaust yourself trying to keep in line with a couple of super-fit neighbours or to be constantly hanging about while some laggard finally catches up with the line: and no need to be permanently alert in case a grouse suddenly springs up forty yards ahead of you. In short: shooting over dogs is a much more relaxing way of hunting grouse than walking in line, so make sure that your guns know it and get full benefit.

Whether the problem of guns wanting to walk in line arises at all will depend largely on how many guns are in the shooting party. Ideally, you would have just two guns, and both would go forward every time a dog came on point. Under those circumstances there is neither the urge, nor the number of bodies available to make walking in line a possibility. It is when you have six or eight guns in the party that problems can arise if you let them. If some or all of the party do decide that they would get more shooting by lining out and walking up, then the best thing you can do is to pick up your dogs, put them on leads, and let the guns get on with walking up. There is no need to fall out over this: it is their shooting day after all, and if they prefer to spend it tramping along in line then that is their privilege. By the same token, if you are not prepared to risk your dogs' discipline and safety by running them in front of a line of guns, then you too are acting within your rights.

If you have more than two guns they should pair off into teams of two and take it in turn to go to a point. They can be very formal about this if they like, sticking rigidly to their teams and their turns, or, as is usually the case, they can become more relaxed as the day goes on and send the fitter guns forward when the dog points on the top of a steep brae face, or cede their turn to someone who has had less shooting over the course of the day. Who goes forward to each point is up to the guns themselves. What you require is simply that, when the dog comes on point, there is a pair of guns ready to come forward and accompany you to where the dog is waiting. An excess of politeness can be something of a nuisance at times, particularly when the

95

birds are a bit jumpy, your dog is on point a couple of hundred yards away, and the guns are settling in for a long discussion about whose turn it is to shoot. But first we have to find some grouse.

While your dogs are quartering you should be the most advanced member of the shooting party, walking a few yards ahead so that the dog can distinguish you easily from the rest of the party. He will be looking to you for directions and encouragement and he needs to be able to see you clearly and quickly without having to search through a knot of people. If you are working unfamiliar ground it may be as well to have the keeper walking with you to show you the limits of the beat. Everyone else should stay a few yards behind and they should stay pretty much together. You don't want them wandering about all over the hill, and though you don't want the whole party right on your heels, neither do you want them lagging a quarter of a mile behind. Things can become a little tense if your dog is on point a couple of hundred yards in front and the guns are out of sight to the rear.

Take care not to be the cause of this happening. You may be extremely fit, but it is possible – even likely – that some of the shooting party will not be. If it is obvious that there are those who are struggling to keep up then adjust your own pace accordingly: bring the dog in for a rest now and again, or call the occasional halt so that everyone can get gathered up and take a breather. After each point take plenty of time to pick up the shot birds and don't be in a great rush to cast the dog off again. You are not competing in a marathon, and most guns would rather cover a bit less ground but do so at a reasonable pace for their level of fitness than try to take in a few more acres and end up totally exhausted by midday.

If there are other dogs among the party you should insist that they are kept under control, either properly at heel or on a lead. Some birddogs can be quite jealous of 'their' birds when they are on point, and seeing another dog running free in the vicinity may be enough to make them go in and flush the covey. For the same reason it is not a good idea for the guns going to a point to bring their dogs forward with them, even if they are completely steady at heel and not liable to run in when a grouse falls. They should either be sat and told to stay, well behind the point, or left with another member of the party holding their leads. It is quite understandable that the owners may want their own dogs to retrieve their birds, but there will be plenty of time for retrieving once the shooting is over.

There may be a vehicle of some kind accompanying the shooting party. Argocats and quad bikes are as common now as the hill pony was in times past, and given a skilful driver they can go almost anywhere that a man on foot is likely to venture. They can be a great help in carrying lunches, coats, spare cartridges, drinks and of course, the shot grouse. It is not unknown for the guns themselves to hitch a lift towards the end of a long day. In one important respect though they are at a disadvantage when compared with a pony. They are all noisy.

The noise may not be particularly loud, but at times it is enough to cause grouse to rise, particularly if the vehicle is brought anywhere near where the dog is on point. It is natural for the driver to want to see what is happening, but it can be fatal for the prospects of sport on a day when the grouse are more than usually skittish. If the wind is blowing strongly into your face as you work the noise will probably not be a problem, but on a still day the buzz of an exhaust can carry a long way across the hill. I'm not suggesting that you should insist on the vehicle staying half a mile to the rear, but, if you find that the birds are not sitting as well as you might expect it is certainly worth asking the driver to hang back a bit more.

Most of the time the ideal way to work a pointer or setter is directly into the wind. At field trials, as we will see in another chapter, the organisers go to a great deal of trouble to ensure that every brace of dogs works into the wind, or as nearly into the wind as is possible. On a shooting day, unless you are very lucky with the lie of the ground, it is highly likely that you

Argocats are useful to carry lunches and spare gear but at times the noise of the engine may spook the grouse.

will have to work upwind, downwind and probably with cheek winds as well. There are all sorts of factors to take into account when organising a day's shooting, and access to the moor, the site of the lunch hut, the need to get vehicles to a particular point or any of a dozen other reasons may dictate how the ground has to be worked. However, it is always worth having a chat with the keeper beforehand, if this is feasible, and trying to ensure that you work the beat in the way that will give your dogs the best chance of finding birds.

You have to be practical about this. Imagine that your beat is a long strip of moorland running east and west along the face of a steeply sloping hill. The wind is blowing directly out of the north and coming straight down the hill. In theory, you might like to work a beat straight up the hill into the wind, then come back to the bottom, move along a couple of hundred yards then take another beat up the hill, and another until you had finished the beat. If you were running in a field trial that is probably how the organisers would do it. It might well be the best way to work the dogs in that they would only hunt directly into the wind. The problem is, your guns are unlikely to take kindly to tracking up and down that hill all day, and when you do reach the far end, having covered the whole beat, they would then have to trek all the way back through ground that has already been worked once that day.

Under those circumstances it is almost certain that you would have to work the beat along its length, going out in the morning along the contours with the wind blowing from one side, then coming back in the afternoon, higher up (or lower down) with the wind on the other cheek. It might not be ideal for the dogs, but it would save the guns an awful lot of needless climbing and allow them to be shooting, or at least hoping for a shot, all the while they were on the hill.

Take another hypothetical situation. Suppose you are going to be dropped off to start work at one point on the moor and picked up later at another point. It may be that, by changing things around and starting the day at the finish point as it were, that you can work into the wind all day long instead of spending the whole day with it at your back. Under this circumstance it would certainly be worthwhile switching the plan around, always supposing that there wasn't some other, more pressing reason, for running with the original plan.

Having tried to ensure that you are giving your dogs and your guns the most favourable conditions that are practical on the day it is up to you to get on with it and make the best of the job. You may be working into the teeth of a gale, or on the sort of day when smoke rises straight up in a thin, unbroken column. It may be raining or sunny, freezing cold or baking hot. There may be lots of grouse or hardly any: they may be sitting so tightly that you have to practically stand on them before they will rise or they may be flushing a quarter of a mile in front of you. Pointers and setters are remarkably adaptable and will do their best to cope with whatever the day throws at them. Once you have ensured that conditions will be as favourable for them as you can arrange on the day the best thing to do is to turn a dog loose and let him get on with it. An experienced dog will know how to adapt his work to the prevailing conditions, and an inexperienced dog, if he has the right potential, will soon learn.

Controlling the Guns

The first priority on any shooting day must be safety. A shotgun is a dangerous weapon and carrying it across rough hill and moorland greatly increases the likelihood of an accident when compared with using it while standing at a peg or in a butt. Stumbling in long heather, stepping into a hidden drainage ditch or tripping on a rock could all lead to a fall and the possibility of an accidental discharge. It doesn't matter that the safety catch is on: with some guns a sharp blow can be enough to trip the sear and fire a cartridge. Add to that the fact that grouse tend to fly close to the ground so that shots are going to be fired horizontally rather than vertically, that they jump suddenly out of the heather and may take off in any direction, and that shots may have to be taken very quickly if the birds are to be in range and it is clear that the potential for having an accident is considerable. Some sensible rules, clearly understood and properly applied are essential for everyone's safety, including your own and that of your dogs.

We have already established that we are shooting over dogs: not walking up grouse in a line. There is no need for a gun to be loaded until a dog comes on to point. Guns should be open and empty right up to the time when your dog says there are birds ahead. There will be plenty of time for the two guns who are going to the point to slip cartridges into the breech as they go forward.

You may be asked whether it would not be better for the party to carry their guns loaded all the while in case they walk up a bird that the dog has missed. There are several reasons why this is not a good idea. For a start, if scenting conditions are reasonable and your dogs are working properly they are not going to miss many birds, if any. The chances are that the shooting party will be carrying loaded guns all day long for no reason. And remember, they should be walking in a group, not spaced out in line, so if one of them does stumble and let off a shot accidentally, there is a very good chance that it will hit one of the others at close range, and an ounce of shot at a range of a few feet can do some absolutely horrific damage to whoever it hits.

There is no need to load and close guns until the dog is clearly on point.

Remember too that you will be controlling your dogs from a few yards ahead of the rest of the party. Do you really want to spend the whole day with two, or four, or perhaps eight loaded guns being lugged along just behind your back? Suppose that the guns do put up a grouse. Its appearance will be sudden and unexpected, and the odds are that if one or more of the party do react quickly enough to shoot it is going to be a snap shot. Are you certain that they are all calm enough to check exactly where you and your dog are before firing, or is someone going to blaze away at the first sight of a grouse and only realise that the dog was in line of fire after it has been shot?

Remember that we want the guns to stay together so as to make the dogs' work simpler. If you allow them to carry loaded guns ready to shoot any stray birds they see the odds are that they will start spreading out across the hill so as to increase their chances of finding a grouse. The next thing is, you are working your dog in front of a line of guns: the very thing you wanted to avoid. So guns should stay empty until a dog is on point. They can even be carried in slips if the guns prefer. It will take a few more seconds to break them out when the dog points, but a gun slip slung over the shoulder is a much easier burden than a gun under the arm. It may not seem heavy or awkward at the start of the day, but after six or seven hours on the hill even a light gun can become surprisingly heavy.

99

When the dog does point, and you are reasonably certain that he is on birds and not just making a cautious investigation of a trace of scent, the first thing to do is to let the guns know that they are in business. If you are walking close to them all you need to do is to turn and say 'He's on'. If they have been taking an interest in the dog work they will probably know that anyway. It may be though, that although you can see the dog he is out of sight of the shooting party. Perhaps he has disappeared over a ridge and not come back and you have gone forward to investigate, or maybe he is pointing in a peat hag where only you can see him. Under these circumstances it is useful to have agreed a hand signal that will allow you to alert the guns without having to bellow the information across the moor. An arm raised vertically is the usual signal and is far less likely to flush the covey than a voice shouting at full pitch.

Gather up your two guns and take them in to where the dog is pointing. This sounds like a simple enough task and on occasion it may be, but it can be made more difficult by several factors. If you are working directly into the wind, if the dog is on point straight in front of you, if you are on reasonably level ground, if the birds are sitting tightly and if the guns have listened to and understood their instructions, then it is – or should be – simply a matter of walking up to the dog with a gun on either side of you, allowing them to take up their positions just ahead of the dog, and then sending the dog forward to flush the grouse. However: you may have noticed rather a lot of 'ifs' in the previous sentence. It is dealing with those 'ifs' that can make it something more than a simple task.

Ideally you will be close alongside the dog with the guns ten to fifteen yards on either side of you and slightly ahead of the dog. When the dog starts to rode in, unless the grouse jump immediately, the guns should go forward as well, maintaining their position beside and slightly ahead of the dog. Then, when the grouse do rise, both guns should be properly placed to take their shots.

Ideally the handler will be alongside his dog with the guns on either side and just in front when the birds rise.

With this gun standing behind the dog and handler his chance of a shot will be lost if the grouse break to the right.

When you start forward to the point it is important that you have the guns alongside you, not behind you. There is a natural desire to get to the dog as quickly as possible, but you must make sure that you aren't tempted to hurry and so get ahead of the guns. If the birds are sitting well they will stay there until you and the guns are in position. If they are jumpy, and liable to rise as you are going in, then you do not want to be so placed that you are blocking the guns' chances of a shot. Nor do you want to rush the guns forward so that they are out of breath and unsteady when the birds jump. Stay calm, take your time, and your attitude will rub off on the guns, the dog and maybe even the grouse. Go rushing forward in a flap and you will have the guns panicking, the dog getting unsettled and the grouse jumping prematurely.

Although you should not rush forward ahead of the guns, it is equally important that they do not go charging in to where the dog is pointing without waiting for you. If the guns are there ahead of you and the birds flush as they arrive, you will not be on hand to ensure that your dog stays steady. If he sees birds rising, hears shots and then sees them falling just ahead of him, and there is no handler close by to restrain him, there is a fair chance that he may decide to run in – and once started, it may be difficult to stop him doing it in future.

Make sure that your guns clearly understand the need to try and take up a position at least level with and preferably ahead of the dog. If a gun is standing fifteen yards behind the point and the grouse are twenty-five yards in front of the dog, then by the time he has seen them flush and mounted the gun they will be out of range. If they are forty yards ahead of the dog – and forty yards is not at all unreasonable when scent is good – then they will be out of range from the moment they leave the ground. Let the guns be just five yards in front of the dog though and they will have a fair chance to kill a bird or a brace even from those birds forty yards ahead of the point. If the birds happen to be right under the dog's nose, then it is a simple matter for the gun to wait long enough for them to get a fair distance away before shooting. If they get up too close you can wait until they are at a sporting distance: if they get up out of range then there is nothing whatsoever you can do, except hope to find the covey again later.

101

Going in to flush with the handler nicely relaxed and allowing the dog to get on with his job.

On a down-wind beat take the guns straight in to the dog. The Labrador should stay until the handler calls him forward to retrieve.

Some guns – usually those who have working dogs of their own – have a natural understanding of what the pointing dog is telling them while others, to put it bluntly, don't seem to have a clue. This is most obvious when the birds don't rise as soon as the dog starts roding in. They may be running or, on a good scenting day, they may just be well ahead of where the dog was on point. The clever gun will watch what the dog is doing and adjust his position accordingly, moving forward or to the side as the dog moves; always keeping in mind where the birds are most likely to rise and where his safe angles of fire lie. Unfortunately not all guns share this instinctive feel for dog work.

All too often the guns seem to require more handling than the dog. Hanging back behind the point, standing still when the dog rodes forward or simply getting into a position where the dog and the handler are between them and the covey are common faults and worse: they are faults that are sometimes repeated time after time on the same day. Some guns listen to instructions, learn from experience and very quickly pick up the requirements of shooting over a pointing dog. Others virtually have to be physically manoeuvred into place – point after point after point. At times this positioning of an apparently reluctant gun can be sheer hard work.

Even so, it is up to you as the dog handler to try to ensure – to encourage, order, cajole, threaten and insist – that the guns are in the best position for a shot at the moment the grouse erupt from the heather. It is not only in the guns' interest: it is very much in the interest of you and your dog as well. Imagine a dog on point on a covey of running grouse. He rodes forward and the guns move with him. Then the grouse turn away to the left: the dog turns with them and the right hand gun takes just a couple of steps forward and then stops. Now, if those grouse get up, you and the dog will be directly between the gun and the covey. If he is a safe, calm

The handler warning the gun that the dog has turned his head and is indicating that the birds have run to the left from the original find.

and sensible gun he will simply have lost his chance of a shot. If he is a bit precipitate; perhaps a little wild or overexcited, then you may feel the wind of a couple of ounces of lead passing close by your ears. And you had better hope that is all you feel.

What should have happened, when the dog swung round to its left, was that the left hand gun should have stayed still, or even taken a couple of steps backwards, while the right hand gun swung round in an arc so that he was again positioned slightly ahead of where the dog was now saying the grouse had gone. You should have steadied the dog and kept a low profile until the right hand gun had got round into his new position, then started the dog forward again. If you happen to be on the track of an old, cock grouse, running through a maze of peat hags, there can be an awful lot of changes of direction before you finally get him on the wing. If you have to spend an inordinate amount of time in positioning and re-positioning the guns there is a good chance that he will eventually rise out of sight, out of range or both.

When a bird, or a covey has got up and given the guns a shot make sure that they reload straight away. There is no law that says every grouse in a covey will rise at the same moment, and many a grouse has had its life saved by the fact that a gun has forgotten to reload after firing his first couple of shots. The pickers-up should keep their dogs at heel until after your dog has cleared the ground – that is to say, gone forward to where the birds rose and checked to see if there are any others still crouching in the heather. Only then should you allow the spaniels or the Labradors to come in and start collecting the dead or wounded.

If there are other birds then a pointer or setter should point them and alert the guns to their presence. If you don't clear the ground properly there is always the chance of a bird jumping while the retrievers are at work and, since the shot birds will probably lie farther out than the sitting birds, there is a danger that a retriever could be shot. This may sound unlikely, but I once saw a spaniel escape a peppering or worse only by blind good luck. The owner was an under-keeper who insisted on sending his spaniel in to retrieve the instant the first grouse hit the heather. I think the reason for this was that the pointers we were working at the time were also somewhat keen on retrieving and he was determined to get as much work as possible for his own dog. On this occasion half the covey had stayed couched in the heather when the first half-dozen birds rose, and as the spaniel ran through them for her retrieve they jumped and flew in the same direction as she was running. The guns hadn't seen the spaniel coming: all they saw was another five or six grouse, and it was a miracle that the little cocker escaped unscathed as shot whistled into the heather all around her. A somewhat white-faced owner was a little more careful about when he released her from then onwards.

Always bear in mind that the purpose for which you are all out on the hill is to shoot grouse, and the reason the guns are doing it is because they expect to enjoy the day. They are not there simply to watch an exhibition of dog work, no matter how fast, wide-ranging and stylish your dogs may be. They are there to shoot grouse. Since they are likely to be spending much of the day watching dogs at work it is to be hoped that they will enjoy and appreciate the spectacle, but remember that the dog work is only a means to an end, and not the end in itself.

I was working a very fast and fit young pointer up in Sutherland one day for a team of guns who, though also young, were neither fast nor fit. We were working the side of a steep hill and the dog was absolutely flying up and down the face. A couple of times he paused on a whiff of scent right at the top of his cast, and each time there was a smothered groan from behind me, followed by a sigh of relief when the dog decided that there was nothing of interest and turned to start back down hill. The third time it happened I heard one of the guns say: 'If that bloody dog had any tact he wouldn't go up the hill…'

It may be an impressive sight to see a pointer or setter quartering high and wide, but if your guns are elderly, not very fit, or simply tired towards the end of a long day, it may be tactful to rein the dog in a little bit: perhaps turn him before he gets too far above you. Admittedly he will cover a bit less ground that way and probably find fewer birds, but provided they are getting a reasonable amount of shooting, there are some guns who would willingly miss out on a couple of shots in return for a day that doesn't involve quite so much mountaineering. Equally, you may find yourself with a few super-fit types who will happily follow the dog to the top of every hill. The question then may be whether you and your dogs are fit enough to keep up with them. Just remember that it isn't a race or a test of endurance. You are there to shoot grouse – and to enjoy yourselves as you do it.

Handling your Dog

It might appear that handling your dog would be the most important thing that you do when you are working pointers and setters for a shooting party, but, depending on the dog, he may need very little actual handling. A good, experienced dog knows what he is meant to do and the best way to do it, and left to himself he will probably work a lot better than if you keep messing him about with unnecessary orders. On the other hand, there are those dogs – and they can be veterans with half a dozen seasons' work behind them just as well as youngsters in their first year – who need to be controlled and directed if they are to work properly. Much the same can be said of handlers. Some handlers like to play an active role, turning their dog with the whistle and sending it here and there with hand signals, while others much prefer to leave it to the dog. Only you can know which particular combination you and your dog together comprise.

It is impossible to set out a strict, or even an approximate, guide to how a pointer or setter should work on a shooting day. There are far too many variables to consider. There is the type of ground you are working, which might be a hard, dry Pennine moor with well-burnt heather and a covey to the acre, or a Sutherland flow mostly covered in deer grass and bog cotton with only the occasional patch of heather to attract grouse. You may be tripping over coveys every few yards or you may have to cover half the county before you find the first barren pair. You may be asked to keep strictly to the boundaries of the beat, or you may be given carte blanche to wander all over the hill, provided that the dog can find some birds.

The birds themselves will have a large say in how the dogs work. They may be sitting tightly or they may have their heads up ready to take off at the first hint of danger. When the dog finds them they may tuck down in the heather or they may run. An individual covey may be gathered together in a few square yards of heather or they may be scattered over the face of the hill. They may rise as a covey with the whole lot getting up at the same time or they may spring in twos and threes. Even when the whole covey appears to have gone off together there may still be an odd bird or two crouching in cover, undecided whether to fly or to hide. Are you out on the hill in August when the young birds are still instinctively hiding from danger, or is it the back end of the season when their first instinct may be to trust their wings to keep them clear of trouble? Can you lead the guns directly up to the point marching boldly across the heather or will they have to creep carefully forward in the cover of a peat hag if they are have any chance of getting within range of the birds before they fly?

And then there is the question of scent. Will your dogs be finding birds with complete assurance or will they be getting little hints of scent, stopping for a few seconds, checking and then moving on a few yards and checking again before finally coming on to a firm point? Can they take in great swathes of hill on each cast or do they have to limit themselves to just a few yards of ground at a time in order not to miss birds? You will have no more than the vaguest of ideas about how good or bad the scent is, but your dog will know and, if he is using his initiative, will adjust his quartering to suit.

Perhaps the best advice I ever heard given to a novice handler came from the late Lord

Joicey: a man with tremendous experience of dogs and grouse. As nearly as I can remember his words they were: 'Take your whistle out of your mouth, put your hands into your pockets, and let the dog get on with his work.' It is advice that anyone working a pointer or setter on a shooting day is well to remember.

I hasten to add that he was not advocating letting the dog simply run wild. Rather, the point being made was that most dogs, given the chance, will settle down into natural rhythm in their running and their quartering and will work better, for longer, if they are allowed to work to this pattern rather than being constantly interrupted by the handler's whistle, voice or hand signals. It may be as well to give the dog a couple of reminders when he is first cast off in the morning, turning him on the whistle at the end of one or two casts, just to let him know that you are still in charge even if you are not constantly nagging at him, but once he settles down to his work *let him get on with it*. He will be all the better for it.

That said, there are some dogs that do require rather more than minimal handling if they are to be kept within bounds. If your dog has that particular stubbornness, or independence of spirit, that drives him to take off into the distance, or to cast wider and wider until he is taking in half the county, then you may need to keep on top of him all the time he is working. Only experience with each individual dog can tell us how he will react on a shooting day, and although most dogs can safely be left to get on with the job there are those that cannot. It doesn't necessarily mean that they are worse at their work than those that can be left alone, but it does mean that they are harder work for the handler.

Unless you are very lucky it is unlikely that you will be able to work your dogs directly into the wind for the whole day. Indeed, there may not be any wind, or what wind there is may be swirling about from all quarters. Even when you are apparently going straight into the wind peat hags and gullies can funnel and twist the breeze so that the actual wind direction at dog level is quite different to what you are feeling in your face six feet above the heather. The wind can curl back up the face of a hill or swirl around the sides of a corrie in quite unexpected ways – ask any deer stalker. Don't be alarmed if at times your dog appears to be working contrary to the way the wind seems to be blowing. Where the wind makes local variations according to the ground a good dog will automatically adjust his quartering to suit.

Working down wind means that your dog is always liable to flush birds before he has the chance to point them, no matter how he adjusts his pattern to cope with the conditions. The classic method of working down wind, as neatly drawn out in many an article and book, is for the dog to go straight forward for a considerable distance and then to quarter the ground back towards the shooting party. In theory this is supposed to minimise the chance of a covey being flushed out of range of the guns as, apart from the out run, the dog is always working into the wind. It looks good on paper, and if you have a dog that is inclined to work in that way there is no reason why he should not do it.

According to the theory the handler and the guns should not advance from where they are standing until the dog either points or has worked out all the ground he has taken in on his out run. Then the whole party moves forward to the point from which the dog started working back and the dog is sent off on his next out run, everyone standing still once again until he either points or works back to them. And so ad infinitum, or at least until you reach the end of the downwind beat. There are though a couple of snags with the method.

Unless you and the guns are very well disciplined you are not going to stand and wait patiently while the dog quarters back to you before going forward to where he is next cast off. Your natural inclination will be to walk forward and meet the dog coming back, and in so doing you are liable to walk up birds that are sitting in ground that the dog has not yet covered. Even supposing that you don't do that, what happens if the dog goes out a couple of hundred yards and then points a covey on his first cast? The guns are then going to have to walk right through all the ground between where they are standing and where the dog is pointing, and none of that ground has been worked as yet. If there is another covey between guns and dog there is a good chance the guns will flush them as they go forward.

This presents you with something of a dilemma. If the guns who are advancing towards the pointing dog walk up birds, should they shoot them, or do you instruct them to shoot only those grouse that the dog is actually pointing? The 'correct' answer according to the strict protocol of shooting over pointing dogs is that only birds that have been pointed should be shot. Certainly, if your dog is on point a hundred yards ahead and the guns suddenly start firing at another covey – shots going off, grouse flying and perhaps falling right in front of him – it is going to be a severe test of his staunchness on point and general steadiness. There is also a strong possibility that the covey he is pointing will remember a more pressing engagement elsewhere and exit stage left. So no shooting if the guns walk up birds on their way in to a point.

But wait a moment. How can you be certain that those birds that rise as you take the guns forward are not the covey your dog is pointing? Okay: so he is a hundred yards away, but a good scent, a scattered covey and perhaps a tendency for the birds to run when they are pointed could easily mean that the birds you have just walked up were the same ones that the dog was pointing. And if you have instructed the guns not to shoot them you are not going to be very popular when you get to where the dog is pointing and there are no birds left.

In fact, the way that pointers and setters handle down wind work in practice can differ considerably from the generally advanced theory. While I have no doubt there are dogs that work exactly as per the textbook I must admit that I have never seen one actually doing it when working a down wind beat. On paper those neat lines showing the direction that the dog takes on its out run and then the geometrically perfect pattern as it quarters back to the shooting party are fine, but grouse moors in general are not quite as flat and featureless as the pages of a book. For instance, what do you do if, as is so often the case, you can only see a hundred yards ahead because the ground drops away in front of you? You could still send the dog several hundred yards forward on an out run, but what then? You can't see him, you don't know if he is quartering, pointing, chasing a hare or laying down in the heather and taking a rest. The only way to find out is to walk forward through that ground that hasn't yet been hunted. And suppose you walk up some birds as you go forward? The guns can't shoot because they don't know whether the dog is a quarter of a mile away or just over the brow of the hill directly in line of fire.

A good dog with plenty of experience working down wind will, if left to get on with it, work out his own solution to coping with the conditions. He knows that he is there to find grouse and that if he flushes them wild he hasn't done his job properly. Most of the dogs that I have worked or seen working on down wind beats have quartered their ground in much the same way as if they were working into the wind: crossing back and forth in front of the shooting party with each beat a bit further on than the last. The pattern tends to be less regular. Perhaps the dog picks up little hints of foot scent that tell him there has been a covey feeding in the vicinity. He may then put in a deeper cast so as to get round behind where he thinks the birds will be and then work back into the wind until he finds them. He may just find them and point them in the course of his original pattern. And of course; because this is a down wind beat; there is always the possibility that he will flush birds because he was right among them before he touched any scent.

But let us suppose that he has found some birds and come on to point. The odds are that he is now pointing towards the shooting party and that the covey is somewhere in between you and the

Nothing can compare with the absolute intensity of a dog on point.

dog. This is another moment when what the textbooks advise is not what happens out on the hill. According to the book you should lead the guns off on a wide detour, circling around the dog and eventually coming in from behind, with a gun either side, just as if you had been working into the wind. You just have to hope that the grouse sit patiently while you do this and don't decide to run or fly during the time when you are performing your flanking manoeuvre. Oh yes: and if you and two guns have gone on a lap round the dog, leaving the rest of the shooting party behind, when you eventually get to the point the covey are quite likely to get up directly between the guns and the spectators.

What happens in practice is that the handler and the guns walk straight to where the dog is pointing: the handler going directly towards the dog and the guns spaced out ten to fifteen yards on either side. You will probably walk the birds up as you get near the dog, though there are times, particularly early in the season, when you may walk right through the middle of the covey without flushing them. If you do reach the dog without any birds rising you just turn around and work the point out as if you were going into the wind – but watch out for the rest of the party if they are now in line of fire. If, as is more likely, the grouse rise as you walk up to them the guns simply pick their shots while you make sure that the dog is steady.

Incidentally, if you want photographs of a dog on point, you will get much better pictures on a downwind beat where he is looking straight at you and the camera can capture all the intensity and concentration on his face. You may even get a shot with the grouse rising in the foreground and the guns on either side.

At times the grouse will elect to run off to one side as the guns and handler approach. You can usually tell if this is happening because the dog will turn his head to track the scent. You should be alert to this possibility and ready to change the position of the guns accordingly, otherwise the gun on the far side may be unable to get a shot because you and the other gun are between him and the birds when they rise.

Handling running birds is an art in itself. Early in the season the grouse will usually sit quite tightly when the dog points them, but as autumn advances they are more likely to run before they rise. Old cock grouse, particularly those living on their own, can run like stags, twisting and turning for several hundred yards before electing to use their wings. How well you, the dog and the guns cope with them is largely a matter of experience.

Some dogs, confronted with running birds, will drop their heads and follow the foot scent, just as a spaniel would do. Others, losing the direct body scent as the birds move across the wind, prefer to re-cast themselves, usually just a few yards at a time, and then point the birds again. This is not something that you can teach the dog: just like working down wind, it is something that he will learn for himself as he gains experience. What you may have to do though, particularly if he is following foot scent, is to steady him down so that he doesn't press the birds so hard that they rise out of gunshot. Guns who are reasonably fit and alert to the nuances of the dog are a great help at these times. If you have to continually stop the dog from tracking the birds while you struggle to get a couple of reluctant guns into position you may find that the grouse will either rise out of range or simply disappear among the hags and the heather.

Caught between the guns and the dog, grouse will sometimes sit tighter when on a down-wind beat.

109

If your dog uses the re-cast and point again method of hunting running birds it is still important for the guns to get to the points as quickly as their fitness and safety will allow. Once grouse start running they will probably not stop just because the dog has pointed them for a second, third or tenth time, and if the guns are too slow getting in to the point they may have moved off too far for the dog to go in and flush them directly – which means he will have to re-cast and find them again. This can be exciting for the guns and quite fascinating for anyone interested in dog work, but it can also be frustrating if point after point seems to be blank. Then, suddenly, there are grouse in the air, the dog has that little look about him that says, 'I told you they were there' and the guns have gone from sceptical to admiring all in the space of half a second. Unless, of course, they were too slow, or wouldn't follow orders, and had to watch the grouse get up out of range. If so, you can at least hope they will have learned their lesson ready for the next lot of running birds.

The ability to 'read' your dog is always important, but when working down wind it is even more vital if you are to get the best results for your guns. Because he is working down wind there is always the danger that he will flush birds because he is right in the middle of the covey before he gets any scent from them. If this happens he should drop as soon as the birds rise and stay down until you tell him to get on again. Don't be in too much haste to do this until you have brought the guns up into position because there may well be one or two grouse left behind. If there are the dog may be able to point them, but there is no guarantee that they will sit once he starts hunting, so get your guns up to the dog before you start him off again.

I have owned several dogs that would sometimes drop down into the heather instead of pointing, even though no birds had been flushed. This invariably meant that their quartering had taken them right into the middle of a covey and that, when the guns came forward, the birds could rise from anywhere around the dog. At other times the dog may point as normal, but then turn his head until he is looking almost behind himself. This normally indicates birds that have run past him as the guns approach, but again, it may mean that he is in the middle of a covey and is aware of birds behind him as well as in front. The more you work him in difficult conditions the better you will become at interpreting his body language and understanding what he is telling you in any particular situation. The better you understand your dog the better you can manage your guns: and the more grouse they will shoot. Or shoot at.

There are a whole range of situations between working directly into the wind and working straight down wind, and they are usually referred to as working a cheek wind. Different dogs find different ways to cope with these situations, but as long as your dog is quartering across the breeze it is probably best to remember the original adage and let him get on with it. An experienced dog will know what he is doing: a youngster will learn, in the only way he can, by getting experience. In some ways cheek winds are more difficult for the handler than a straight down wind beat, though the dogs generally cope with them with little trouble.

One problem that can arise is that the dog will tend to turn a cheek wind into a head wind as he quarters across the breeze. Picture a situation where you are heading due north along your allotted beat with the wind coming from the west and blowing on your left cheek. You set the dog off and he goes out across the wind which means he sets off in the same direction as you are heading. A couple of hundred yards out he turns to his left and comes back towards you on a parallel heading. After three or four casts he will be a hundred yards or more off to your left and you will have advanced to about the position where he ended his first cast and started back towards you.

At this point you should recall the dog and start him off on a new beat ahead of you. If you keep walking forward you will be advancing into ground that has not yet been hunted. The natural tendency for your dog though is to carry on working into the wind, so this is one

Grouse don't always offer simple, going-away shots. These have broken back and the handler looks to be in some danger.

Taking a break on the hill with a motley crew of Pointers and Cocker Spaniels.

situation when you will need your whistle to bring him back down your end of the beat. When he finds birds you will, naturally, have to go to the point. Let us suppose that he finds a covey well out on your left. You take the guns in, they fire a few shots, the retrievers come up and collect the birds and then – what? If you cast off from where you are each time there is a point you are going to gradually move farther and farther to the west and away from your original line. This may not matter, but if you are on a moor where the keeper wants you to keep fairly closely to a particular beat you may have to keep bringing the party back onto the original line of march to prevent a steady westwards creep taking you into the wrong ground.

When working cheek winds some dogs seem to favour one side more than the other: in other words, they will cast out a couple of hundred yards on (say) your left, but turn almost as soon as they have gone out to the right. Or, of course, vice versa. You can cope with this in two ways. One is to get your whistle out and insist on the dog working full distance on either side of the beat – always assuming that he is sufficiently responsive to the whistle and to hand signals to do this. An alternative strategy is to adjust your own positioning to take account of the dog's eccentricity.

If he is working well out in front and to your left say, (on a wind coming from ahead and to the right), but not doing much behind and to the right, then by walking along the right hand boundary of the beat you will have him covering the whole of the ground without a lot of handling on your part. This is your choice to make of course: you may prefer to insist on his working roughly equal beats on either side of you. From the point of view of discipline and control this is probably the better solution, but if you are confident in your dog and in his ability there is also a lot to be said for letting him do things his way when you can do so without spoiling the prospects of sport for the shooting party.

The amount of leeway you allow your dogs to take and the degree to which you should let them set the bounds of their beat depend largely on the amount of experience the dogs have already. A young dog in his first season is better kept under control and perhaps even given the occasional unnecessary command just to remind him that he is working for you and not simply out to please himself. If you have used a check cord during training there may be a case for letting a young dog trail a few yards of light line behind him when he is first worked on the hill. Provided there is nothing on the end to get snagged in the heather or on rocks the line shouldn't slow him down, but it will act as a reminder that he is working under orders. It can also be very handy for you to get hold of the line when he is on point and ensure that he stays steady as you and the guns come in over those last few, vital yards. He may not need it – shouldn't need it if you have done your work properly in training – but having that line in your hand is a great confidence booster in the early days of a pup's career.

When the heather is wet the grouse are often reluctant to sit and will raise their heads when the dog points and start moving away. Once you see their heads above the heather you can pretty much guarantee that those grouse will not hang around for very much longer. If they are comfortably within range of the guns then there is no problem, but if you spot birds with their heads up while you are still out of range it is as well to send the guns on as quickly as possible. The dog has done his job and you don't need him to tell you where the birds are anymore: you can see them. If they don't rise – unlikely – and tuck down into the heather out of sight you can always let the dog point them again.

There are times, late in the season when the birds are jumpy and scent is good, that a down wind beat may be the best way to get your guns in range of the coveys. If the birds are getting up before you can reach the point on a normal, into the wind beat it can be almost impossible to get the guns within range. On a down wind beat though the birds are generally sandwiched between the guns and the dog and at times they will sit just that little bit longer and allow you

Reading the dog. The gun adjusts his position as the dog rodes in through short heather.

Irish Setter cooling off in a burn after a long hot day working on the hill.

113

to get your guns close enough for a shot. There are other times though when no matter how quietly and carefully you creep in to the point, the birds simply won't sit. The guns may prefer to try walking up and it is possible that they may have better luck if they do. Otherwise you can just persist and hope that there will be a few birds that sit tighter than the rest.

Working your dogs can mean glorious sunny days with the taste of pollen on your lips, or soaking wet misery as the rain lashes across the hill. You will meet shooting parties that are a pleasure to work with and, if you are unlucky, perhaps a few that are just the opposite. There will be days when the dogs work well and you go home glowing with satisfaction and pride in your protégés and, if you work them often enough, there will inevitably be those other days, when nothing goes right. However many times you go to the hill with a team of pointers or setters there is always something new to learn and something different to see. The experience may not always be quite what you had hoped, but it is what your dogs were bred to do, and several hundred years of breeding have gone into making sure that they can do it as well as possible. I never tire of the experience, good days or bad, and I cannot commend it too highly to you and your own pointers or setters. Nothing else comes close.

CHAPTER 8
Field Trials

If it were not for the Trials, the pointers and setters of today both in this country
and abroad would be in danger of losing all their beautiful style and character,
and every endeavour should be made to avoid this...
Colonel Hubert M. Wilson, writing in *Hounds and Dogs*, The Lonsdale
Library,1943

The first field trial for pointers and setters is generally accepted to have taken place in 1865. Indeed, this was the first official field trial of any kind since trials for spaniels and retrievers did not begin for another thirty odd years. In the one hundred and forty years since then field trials have spread all over the world with the format being adapted to suit conditions in the various countries where they are now held.

It is, I suppose, a logical result of the natural competitive instinct of the human race that some owners should want to test their gundogs against other owners' protégés. The show ring is available for those who want their dogs judged on their looks alone whereas field trials test the working ability of the gundog breeds. It is open to debate how well either form of competition acts in the best interests of the breeds involved, but that particular argument has been on-going for at least a hundred years and will probably continue as long as there are dog shows and field trials in which working gundogs can compete.

Consider the quote from Colonel Wilson that I have used to head this chapter. Having begun by writing: 'If it were not for the Trials, the pointers and setters of today both in this country and abroad would be in danger of losing all their beautiful style and character, and every endeavour should be made to avoid this...' he goes on to add: 'by reducing expenses, encouraging trials for stamina, holding them if possible in August and September and therefore making them correspond more closely to ordinary shooting conditions.'

The second half of the sentence neatly summarises the problem of trying to classify gundogs according to their ability. The original aim of both dog shows and field trials was to compare the merits of working gundogs. However, once a form of competition exists it does not take long before some owners are selecting and breeding for those particular characteristics that tend to win competitions. We have already looked at the factors that led to the separation of nearly all gundog breeds into show types and working types. Beyond that there is a further, though less pronounced, sub-division into working dogs and trialling dogs.

This divide is nowhere near as absolute as that between the working and the show strains of pointers and setters. Any dog with the ability and the training to compete in a field trial also has the ability and the training to work in the shooting field. And though the majority of shooting dogs do not compete in field trials there are plenty that could do so with distinction if their handlers had the time and the inclination to enter them. At the other end of the spectrum many of the regulars on the field trial circuit do take their dogs shooting when the season begins. However, it is quite possible to enter, compete and win at pointer and setter field trials with a dog that has never actually worked for the gun and to make up to field trial champion a dog that has never been taken out on a shooting day.

In all the other field trial disciplines – for spaniels, retrievers and the hunt, point and retrieve

Pointer and setter trials can be run during the close season. Competitors well wrapped up for a spring trial in Perthshire.

breeds – game is actually shot in the course of the trial, so even if the dogs competing are reserved specifically for trialling, the trial itself is still a shooting day. At pointer and setters trials it is practically unknown for birds to be shot. (I say 'practically unknown' because there is nothing in the regulations that says no birds will be shot, and a few years ago, when the Champion Stake took place on the Twelfth of August, grouse were shot over the dogs. The experiment was not a great success and has not been repeated, though an international competition between England, Ireland and Scotland took place at Balmoral a few years ago and was organised as a proper shooting day, with considerable success.) Normally though, no birds are shot, although shots are fired over the dogs to check that they are steady under fire and not gun-shy.

The fact that no birds are killed in the course of a pointer and setter trial means that stakes can be organised outside the shooting seasons. The spring trials are run on grouse in Scotland and on partridge in England during March and April and the summer trials on grouse begin in mid-July and usually end a day or so before grouse shooting starts on the Twelfth of August. During the autumn circuit in September it would be legally possible to shoot partridges (though not pheasants) but at the present time it is not done.

There are certain advantages in having a trial format that does not include the killing of game. Since no birds are killed it is possible to run trials during the close season when the dogs are not scattered on moors throughout the country working for shooting parties. (One of the main reasons why trials were first arranged during July and early August was because all the dogs were working dogs and would be needed elsewhere when the shooting season opened.) It is also easier to persuade a shoot owner to offer his ground for a trial when he knows that his stock is not going to be depleted, and because no birds are shot a trial can still be run on ground where a poor breeding season means that no shooting is planned for that year. Running out of season means that trial dates will not clash with shooting dates and the summer grouse trials can be useful to give the keeper or shoot owner an idea of how well his birds have fared during the breeding season.

The fact that no birds are shot at the trials means that a pointer or setter owner who enjoys dog work but is, shall we say ambivalent, about the killing of game, can still take part without compromising their ideals. It is a moot point whether this is a good thing or not. On the one hand it allows access to the sport for those who might otherwise feel unable to compete on moral grounds, but it also means that handlers and trainers can both run their dogs in and, in some cases, even judge field trials despite having no experience or understanding of the sport of game shooting.

Whether you regard this as an excellent example of inclusivity, or as an unfortunate consequence of running trials during the close season will probably depend on your perception of the purpose and importance of field trials. If you regard a field trial as a means to an end, the 'end' in this case being to improve the working ability of the breeds, then you are likely to feel that a clear understanding of shooting is essential in order to properly work, and far more importantly, to judge, a pointer or setter. If though, you view the competition as an end in itself, as is almost inevitable if your interest is solely in trialling and not in shooting, then I doubt if you will have any problem with the concept.

The stated purpose of a field trial in the Kennel Club regulations is to discover the dog which, on the day, most pleases the judges from a shooting point of view. The problem – if there is a problem – is that a field trial is unable, for several reasons, some voluntary and some unavoidable, to accurately reproduce the format of a day shooting over pointers or setters. Some aspects of their work are reasonably well reflected within the trial format but others simply cannot be tested given the current field trial format. Not surprisingly, the dogs that win trials are those that perform best in the areas of their work that are displayed during the trial. Whether these same dogs would be the best dogs on a proper shooting day is the subject of a discussion that has been going on for at least the last hundred years. It is unlikely that even another hundred years would settle the debate, but that is no reason why we should not explore the arguments.

Consider the opinion of Mr G. T. Teasdale-Buckell, written in 1907 in his book *The Complete Shot* (Methuen)

> *For the last forty years there have been held public field trials on game for pointers and setters. Whether these events have been worked off upon paired partridges in the spring, or contested by finding young broods of grouse just before the opening of the season, they have given breeders and sportsmen the chance of breeding by selection for pace, nose, quartering, and breaking. Unfortunately they have left out stamina. There have been what were at the time called 'stamina trials' but as they were sometimes won by slow dogs they did not merit the high-sounding title, and for real stamina trials one has to go to America.*
>
> *Trials for ability to stay are much more necessary now than ever before, because the dog shows have ceased to be any assistance to breeders of working dogs. When it was possible to compare at shows the external forms of pointers and setters that had succeeded at field trials, they were of some use, on the ground that true formation is suggestive of stamina. But since separate breeds of dogs have been evolved by the shows for the shows, the working dogs are either not sent to them, or do not win if they are sent, so that a show-winning pointer or setter is taken to be bad and of a degraded sort unless the contrary is proved. This is a great pity, for there is no doubt that stamina is the foundation of almost every other virtue in the pointer or setter.*

Those words were written less than fifty years after the first field trial and the first dog show were held and already the writer was lamenting the divide between show dogs and working

The gun at a trial will normally only be fired in order to check the dog's reaction to the sound of a shot.

dogs, and arguing that field trials were not properly representative of a shooting day. Neither was this some maverick opinion offered by an unsuccessful competitor on the trial circuit. Colonel C. J. Cotes, a celebrated gundog breeder, once wrote to Teasdale-Buckell in the following terms: 'I have always considered you to know more about the breaking and breeding of setters than any man living, and that it was entirely through you that the apex of setter breeding was reached about twenty-five years ago...' It is hard to imagine a more ringing endorsement.

So how much have things changed in the hundred years that have passed since then? There is no doubt that the divide between show and working pointers and setters has widened, as is the case with practically all the gundog breeds. As far as differences between trialling and working dogs go it is more difficult to comment since there is no-one still living who could have observed field trials at the turn of the nineteenth and twentieth centuries. In order to better understand the gap between working and trialling we should perhaps begin by looking at the way in which a pointer and setter field trial is organised in Britain today.

When I first took an interest in pointer and setter trials in the early 1970s interest in the sport was lower than it is at present and you were practically guaranteed a run in any stake you entered. Trialling is undoubtedly popular and attracts bigger fields today, though this does not necessarily mean that there are more working pointers and setters in the country. Over the past thirty years both vehicles and the road system have improved considerably and it is now much easier to travel the long distances that may be involved in getting to trials. In addition most employees are entitled to far longer holidays than was the case a few years ago, so taking time off to run in the trials may not mean using up the whole of your holiday allowance for those handlers who work office or factory hours.

As more entrants have sought places for their dogs so it has become more difficult to get a run in a stake, particularly if you have several dogs that you would like to enter. Most stakes are now fully subscribed with several dogs in reserve in case any of the original entry drop out, and this means that around forty to forty-five dogs will be lining up to take part on a typical trial day. One or two stakes are run per day. Open and All-aged stakes normally have a full day allotted, but sometimes a Puppy and a Novice stake will be run on the same day, or perhaps a Breed stake (limited to entrants from a single breed) may be doubled up with one of the former. Entry to Open and All-aged stakes is limited by qualification with all entrants being required to have won an award at a Puppy, Novice or Breed stake before they will be eligible to run at the higher level.

The format for all stakes is pretty much the same. A draw is held, sometimes on the morning of the trial and sometimes the evening before, to determine the running order of the dogs. Numbered armbands are issued, everyone proceeds from the meet to the trial ground and things get under way.

The dogs are always run as a brace: that is two dogs at a time, never singly. The two judges, usually accompanied by the keeper to direct them, call the first pair of competitors forward: handshakes, greetings and good wishes are exchanged, and then the dogs are cast off. They will then run until the judges decide they have seen enough and ask the handlers to pick up. The judges will confer on the work they have just seen and then call for the next pair of contestants to come forward for their turn, and so on until every dog has had a run. The judges then retire to compare notes and decide how many of the first round competitors they want to run again in a second round. After that there may be a third, and occasionally even a fourth round before the judges decide on their winners. Somewhere along the line there will be a break for lunch.

Up to forty-five dogs may take part in a pointer and setter stake.

Given that the trial is unlikely to get under way before ten o'clock and will probably be finished before five o'clock, and allowing an hour in total for lunch, the judges conferring between rounds and the prize-giving at the end, it is unlikely that more than six hours will be spent actually running dogs – and this is a generous estimate. If there are twenty brace in the first round and ten brace in the second, then the average time available for each brace is only twelve minutes, and that twelve minutes includes the time spent swapping over between each pair of contestants and any time the judges spend in discussion between each run. In practice it is not unusual for the entire first round of twenty brace of dogs to be completed in well under three hours with the average length of time for a brace to actually spend running being no more than five or six minutes.

This shortage of time is often compounded by the insistence of trial organisers that dogs will only be run directly into the wind. This is not something that is stipulated in the regulations: indeed, the rules distinguish between flushing into the wind (which is an eliminating offence) and *not dropping to* a downwind flush (my italics), thus making it clear that whoever wrote the regulations understood that the occasional flush when working downwind is unavoidable, and by implication acknowledged that downwind work could take place during a trial. These days it never does and a great deal of time is wasted when, having worked a beat the length of the moor, the whole circus: judges, handlers, dogs, stewards and gun: all troop back over the ground they have just covered and then head back into the wind on a parallel beat. A great deal of the little time available is sometimes spent on these unnecessary excursions when the dogs could just as easily be worked back with the wind behind them.

Competitors collecting their armbands and checking the draw prior to the Champion Stake.

Julie Organ and Dennis Longworth writing up their books during judging for the 2002 Champion Stake.

It is perhaps not entirely fair to look at average running times, because dogs that commit a fault – flush birds, chase hares or otherwise misbehave – may be eliminated within minutes or even seconds of starting their run, thus leaving more time available for the better dogs. Against that must be weighed the occasions when the judges elect to 'protect' the dogs that have performed well in the first round by running them for the shortest possible time in the second and any subsequent rounds. The justification usually given for this is that they do not want to risk the best dogs being eliminated if they make a mistake in the latter part of the trial.

I once watched this policy being taken to quite ludicrous lengths during the course of a Champion Stake. Conditions were difficult: there were a lot of grouse on the moor, scent appeared to be patchy, and a number of dogs were eliminated during the first round when they missed or flushed birds. The second round saw several more dogs dropped and the judges then called eight (if my memory is correct) dogs forward for a third round. The first brace was sent off but as soon as the dogs started to cross in front of their handlers after their initial cast the judges ordered them picked up.

The spectators assumed that the judges had spotted some error unseen by the gallery and eliminated both runners. The puzzled looks and expressions of sympathy had hardly begun before exactly the same thing was done with the second brace, then the third and the fourth. By this time it had become clear that the judges had decided to run a third round, but were so determined not to lose any more of their top runners that they were going to cut each run short before anything could go wrong.

It seemed logical that, having got through that little charade the results would then be announced, but the judges had different ideas. The same runners were called back, in different pairs, for a fourth round. I was standing close enough to hear one of the judges give his instructions to the first brace. 'Cast off,' he said, 'and then see how quickly you can pick them up again.'

121

Each of the four brace then did exactly the same thing. The handlers cast off their dogs, grabbed for their stop whistles and dropped the dogs within ten yards of the release point. They then put on their leads and led them back to where the gallery was looking on with puzzled expressions. The trial was then over, the winners were announced and the awards presented. So why did the judges bother with the little farce at the end?

Afterwards I discussed what had happened with several of the most experienced field trial competitors and found them generally just as confused as I was by what had happened. The consensus was that the judges, for reasons that never became clear, were determined to run four rounds, but equally determined not to have to eliminate any more of the dogs. Certainly four rounds were run – in theory – but in practice there was nothing in either the third or the fourth round that could have had any bearing on the judges' decision as to the winners. They must therefore have already decided their order of merit by the end of the second round. Why they didn't pack up then and announce the result is beyond me though I assume they must have had something in mind.

I, rather naively, suggested to one of the competitors that a better way to complete the trial would have been to give each brace a twenty minute run with instructions to just get on and work their dogs as if they were out shooting. There was plenty of time and ample ground and I felt that this would have been a real test of their respective merits and even allowed us to get an idea of their stamina. He was horrified. 'You couldn't do that,' he said. 'You'd end up with no dogs left.'

To me, the suggestion that, of the eight dogs considered potential winners of the Champion Stake, not one could be expected to run for twenty minutes on a grouse moor in early August without committing an eliminating fault was a poor reflection of the confidence that an experienced handler had in the quality of trialling dogs. Personally, I have little doubt that most if not all eight were more than capable of putting on a really impressive display of dog work and that running them in that manner would have not only produced a winner but would have enabled that dog to really show us what he was capable of doing.

The question of how long a dog should run during a trial in order that a fair assessment can be made of its working ability is something that has concerned commentators ever since field trials began. Colonel Hubert Wilson had this to say on the subject.

Some of the old records as to this question of stoutness are interesting. For instance at Bala in 1867, the trials were run in three hour heats, and at Vagnol in 1870 comment was made on the fact that one dog was only down for one hour while a bitch, Ruth, ran for a full two hours. In 1873 when trials were help at Orwell in September, all dogs had to be down for at least three-quarters of an hour under the judges, Mr Shirley and Mr Lort, who were shooting.

One fact that is evident from the above is that there were far fewer entrants in the trials in those early years. To run all dogs 'for at least three-quarters of an hour' in a modern trial would mean that a first round of twenty brace would take fifteen hours to complete. If the trials were run in three hour heats as they were in 1867 then two brace per day would be the limit and the first round of a trial might drag on for ten days. I suspect that there would be very few landowners, judges or even competitors who could allot that amount of time to a single field trial competition.

The question of whether a pointer or setter can really demonstrate its full ability in the very restricted time available at a field trial has been around for a very long time and will probably continue to be asked as long as trials are run. There is no doubt that the present format of pointer and setter trials precludes any real assessment of stamina being made, despite this being

One thing a field trial cannot test is a dog's stamina. This Irish Setter looks quite fresh despite just having run.

an essential ingredient in the make-up of a working dog, but it is hard to see how this situation can be changed without severely restricting the number of competitors taking part.

If the maximum number of dogs allowed to compete in a one day trial was restricted to ten brace, then it would be possible to run them in thirty minute heats and still complete the first round in five hours. In practice the time needed would almost certainly be less than five hours because dogs committing eliminating faults would be discarded before their half-hour was up. However, there is an important corollary to this proposition. If the number of competitors is restricted then competition for places is also restricted and a win is thus devalued. First among twenty bears less kudos than first among forty – particularly if the best of the competition has failed to make it through the draw for places. Under the present system, at Open stake level, the winner will usually have beaten the best of the field trial dogs in the country. Additionally, restricting the number of entrants would probably result in a number of trainers abandoning field trials, which would also limit the level of competition.

Overall I would suggest that the present format of pointer and setter trials is a reasonable compromise. Anyone who wants to take part is pretty much guaranteed a place in Puppy and Novice stakes and has a very good chance of making the draw in Open and All-aged competition once they have qualified their dog to run. And while stamina is undeniably a vital ingredient in a pointer or setter there are other talents such as quartering, pace, nose, bird-handling ability and style that can be, and are, tested in field trial competitions.

A field trial is supposed to simulate a shooting day, but the organisers of a field trial for pointers and setters are faced with a number of problems that would not normally concern a shoot manager. The ground has to be accessible: not just for a couple of Land Rovers with guns and dogs, but for all the vehicles with competitors, spectators, judges, stewards and keepers and when they get to the trial ground there has to be somewhere to park all the competitors' vehicles.

Billy Darragh and Bob Truman. Trial ground must be open enough to allow judges and handlers to see the dogs easily.

Anywhere that is particularly steep is ruled out because some of those taking part will not be in the first flush of their youth and may not relish bagging a couple of Munros in the course of the morning. It is also best if the judges can actually see the dogs when they are working, so the type of moor that is riven with gullies and peat hags, blind brows and hidden valleys can also be ruled out. Because pointer and setter trials are invariably run directly into the wind the moor must lend itself to being worked in whatever direction the wind is coming from on the day of the trial. Long, narrow moors that can only be worked along their length are out as well. And finally, there has to be a reasonable stock of game.

The spring and autumn trials, held on farmland rather than moorland, are less problematic as regards terrain, but the organisers always have the worry of whether the spring corn/autumn stubbles will be long enough to hold birds at the point and, once again, whether the stock of game will be sufficient for the judges to award a game certificate. While it is evident that it would be impossible to judge a trial if there was no game for the dogs to hunt, it is also true that too much game can also present judges and competitors with problems. If the dogs are tripping over birds every few yards it becomes impossible for them to demonstrate their skill at quartering, nor indeed their game finding ability if all they have to do is adopt a pointing attitude and then rode forward a few yards until they hit the inevitable covey of grouse.

But let us assume that all the organisation has been done, that you have trained your dog to the standard where you believe he is worthy of showing off his paces in public, and you would like to enter him in a trial. How do you proceed?

All pointer and setter field trials are organised by clubs licensed to do so by the Kennel Club, or by the Kennel Club itself. If you contact the field trial secretaries of these clubs they will provide you with the details of the trials they are organising, a schedule setting out where and when the trial will take place, who is judging and stewarding, what the criteria are for entry and usually a list of the prizes on offer, and any local rules and regulations besides. In most cases there are reduced entry fees for club members, plus preferential status if the trial is over-subscribed and nowadays you may have to be a member of the club in order to have any real hope of getting a run.

The best way to start for anyone interested in taking part in pointer and setter field trials is to go along to a trial, watch the action and talk to some of the competitors. This will give you a good idea of the sort of standard you should be aiming for with your own dog and also probably enable you to meet some of those field trial secretaries from the clubs. Give them your name and address and they will be happy to send you membership forms and arrange for you to join. The cost is modest, usually only £5 or £10 per year, though it can mount up if you decide to get seriously involved in trialling and join a number of clubs.

The etiquette involved in trialling is simple and obvious. Take note of your place in the draw and make sure that you are standing by, readily available, when the steward asks you to make your way up to the judges. If you are carrying a stick leave it with one of the spectators while you are running your dog. Sticks are not allowed (though if you genuinely need a stick to walk the judges can make an exception). They will check the number on your armband against their list of runners and confirm that the dog you have brought forward appears to be the one listed in the catalogue. A handshake and a polite greeting to both judges, the same to your running mate, and then listen to any instructions that the judges may give you. This may seem like stating the blindingly obvious, but it is also a good idea to act on those instructions. If you are told that your beat runs in a particular direction, then make sure you head in that direction. It is not at all unusual to see even the most experienced trial competitors listen attentively and nod politely as the judges give their instructions and then blithely set their dogs off in a different direction altogether.

Casting off in fine style to begin their run.

Richard MacNicol going in to a point on the edge of the moor.

But of course you are not going to do that. When the judges indicate that they are ready to begin take your position on either the left or the right according to the number on your armband. The lower number of the brace goes on the left and should send their dog towards the left hand side of the beat on his first cast. Tell the dog to 'Hup', remove the lead and put it in your pocket, look across to make sure that your running mate is also ready to cast off, wish him or her 'Good luck' and then send your dog away.

What should happen now is that you and your fellow competitor walk together along the centre of the beat while your dogs quarter the ground, each on the opposite tack as it were, crossing neatly in front of you at the mid-point of each cast. There are plenty of nice diagrams in books about birddogs and field trials that will show you exactly how this should look using patterns of lines weaving to and fro across the page. Out in the field things are rarely that simple: one dog may be a bit faster than the other, or take a bigger bite of ground when he casts forward, or go further out on the sides of the beat. If things work out like the diagrams in the book then great: if not, just concentrate on what your dog is doing and try to make sure that he does it right.

But don't concentrate entirely and exclusively on your dog. Remember that you are running as one half of a brace, so also try to keep half an eye on what your running mate is doing. If he stops to answer a call of nature (the dog: not, we trust, the handler) it is considered polite to drop your own dog and wait until both are ready to resume. If the other dog comes on to point you can either drop your dog or, if you are confident that he will do it, let him run on until he sees and backs the pointing dog.

A good natural back will earn him more credit from the judges than if you drop him. However, if you allow him to keep running and he doesn't back the pointing dog he will be marked down. If he steals the point or flushes the birds he will be eliminated. It's your decision.

You may be wondering how you are going to both handle your own dog and keep a watch on his brace mate who may be several hundred yards away on the opposite side of the beat. In theory they should be crossing each other at regular intervals: in practice they may well be running close together at times anyway. Usually, when one dog comes on to point someone – the handler, one of the judges or the steward of the beat – will quietly inform the other handler that his running mate is pointing if he appears not to have noticed.

But of course, it may be your dog that finds birds rather than his brace mate. What do you do when he comes on to point?

The first thing is to be sure that he really is pointing and hasn't just stopped to check out a whiff of scent before moving on again. Some dogs seem to have the knack of pointing when and only when they are certain that they have birds, others will flash on to point for a few seconds as they hit a bit of scent then, having satisfied themselves that there are no birds in front of them, will break away and get back into their quartering. He's your dog: it's up to you to read him. You won't impress the judges if you keep claiming a point and then changing your mind after a couple of seconds or so, but unless you are absolutely sure that your dog has birds it won't hurt to give him a few moments before you claim. If there are birds in front of him he won't be going anywhere.

To claim a point you signal by sticking your arm up in the air and turning to the judges to ensure that they are aware of the situation. One of the judges, plus the man who is carrying the gun will then accompany you to where your dog is pointing. Wait until the judge asks you to carry on, then rode the dog in to flush the bird, or birds. When they get up the dog should drop, or at least sit, and the gun will fire a shot into the air. After a short pause the judge will invite you to work out the point. Send your dog on again until he either points more birds from the original covey or indicates that they have all gone. Drop him and wait for orders from the judge, which will probably be to put him on his lead. Don't touch him or put the lead on until asked to do so by the judge.

Grouse away from Colin Organ during the 2000 Champion Stake.

The right hand dog has pointed grouse and the left hand dog is backing him as the handlers go to their dogs.

If nothing has gone wrong the judges will either bring you and your running mate back together and ask you to cast off again, or they will let you know that they have finished with you for the moment. If your brace mate has committed an eliminating fault they may bring a bye dog in and run you on with him, or they may call for the next brace but ask you to stay close by because they may want to see you again. Whatever the outcome you should thank the judges at the end of your run and either go back among the rest of the spectators or, if you have been put on standby, hang around discreetly, far enough behind so as to not interfere with the next dogs to run.

There is, of course an alternative scenario, when things have not gone according to the book. The procedure is much the same. Pick up your dog and put him on his lead, thank the judges and return to the gallery. Rest assured that you will not be alone in falling by the wayside, whatever the reason for your elimination – and there are quite a few possibilities.

Certain faults are defined in the regulations as eliminating faults, and if your dog commits one of these then, in accordance with those regulations he will be eliminated from the trial. These include chasing fur or feather, flushing birds upwind, missing game on the beat, whining or barking, blinking a point, unsteadiness to game and running out of control. Then there are what the Kennel Club describes as major faults: missing birds, not dropping to shot, being sticky on point, failure to quarter and cover the ground properly, persistent false pointing, noisy handling and failing to drop in the event of a downwind flush. In practice, if your dog commits one of the major faults he will be eliminated just as surely as if he had committed one of the specified eliminating faults.

A criticism sometimes levelled at field trial judges is that they engage in 'negative judging'. The implication of such criticism is that, rather than trying to find the dog with the greatest ability they judge by looking for transgressions against the regulations that will allow them to eliminate dogs from the trial. Then, once every dog that has broken a rule, no matter how trivial the offence, has been rejected the winners can be selected from among the dogs that are left – if any.

The Kennel Club's own regulations state that 'the judges should be looking for credit qualities rather than trying to eliminate dogs' but in practice any fault tends to result in elimination for the perpetrator. This approach can be justified in a number of ways. As we have already seen, with forty dogs to be assessed in a single day there is only a very limited amount of time available to look at each competitor. If a dog has committed an error that will effectively rule it out of the awards then why should the judges spend any more time with it? Secondly, by adopting a ruthless attitude to any transgression, no matter how trivial, trainers are encouraged to aim for the highest possible standards from their dogs. Nothing concentrates the mind better than being asked to 'Pick up please' thirty seconds into your run after you have spent a lot of time and money on entering and travelling to the trial. Thirdly, eliminating the 'poorer' dogs quickly leaves more time for looking at the 'better' dogs. And finally, if you throw out every dog that commits any fault, however minor, you cannot be accused of inconsistency in your judging.

Incidentally, this negative approach is in direct contrast to the way in which Hunt, Point and Retrieve trials used to be judged. (I say 'used to be' because the Kennel Club have been making some efforts to force the organisers to change.) There, every dog, provided that it didn't commit a true eliminating fault, was given a full run, even when the work was not of a particularly high standard. One of the senior HPR judges once explained this to me by saying that an extended run gave them the chance to assess the dog properly as well as giving the entrants value for the time, effort and money spent on preparing for the trial. If, in the course of that run their dog made errors, then those errors would be taken into account when the winners were being decided.

In many ways this seemed to me to be a better way of judging. It gave the judges the chance to balance good against bad in the dogs' work, and it also gave each competitor a fair run in return for their entrance fees. Against that, it was clear that the standard of work in HPR trials was often very low, and worse, some of the competitors seemed to be blithely unaware that there was anything wrong with the way their dogs were performing. Disappointing as it undoubtedly is to be thrown out after just a couple of casts there is no doubt that it motivates you to try harder next time. If you have had your full run in both rounds but fail to feature among the awards you can easily convince yourself that you were just unlucky, or that the judges were biased, or that you were pipped to a place by a dog that was just marginally better on the day. Get thrown out early and you know that you have to improve. But let us get back to pointer and setter trials and the problem with negative judging.

That problem, for me, is that the business of eliminating dogs as soon as they are at fault is sometimes taken to extremes. Let us look at a couple of examples. If a dog runs in when birds are flushed he should be eliminated: no question. But what if takes just one step forward: perhaps to see where the birds are going if they swing to one side and the handler is blocking his view? Should he be thrown out for 'running in' in that case? Under some judges he will be. And then there is the matter of missing birds.

A dog quarters his ground, doesn't find anything, and then his brace mate points a covey in the ground he has just been over, or perhaps the handlers, following along behind, walk birds up. He's missed birds and he's out: once again, no question. But suppose he is casting well out to the side and he bangs on to point. It takes a few minutes for handler, judge and gun to get across to him: he rodes in and produces a bird from right in front. As it rises a second birds lifts a few feet behind where he is pointing. Is that really a missed bird, or is it an old cock that has run back behind the dog while he was fully committed to pointing the hen? Many – perhaps most – pointer and setter judges will eliminate a dog when that happens though, out in the shooting field there would be no complaints.

We can make a similar distinction when it comes to eliminating dogs for flushing upwind. A dog is quartering his ground and as he gallops along a covey gets up twenty yards upwind of him. An upwind flush is an eliminating fault and so out he goes. But what if it is a wet day and an old cock grouse rises from a rock where he has been sitting watching procedures for the last twenty minutes? Not so much a flush by the dog as an old bird deciding that the neighbourhood is getting a bit too crowded and now is the time to glide over and inspect the heather on the other side of the valley. On this occasion the dog is not really at fault but he is liable to be eliminated anyway.

Then there is the matter of dropping to shot. Some dogs do drop flat when a shot is fired, others sit and a few may stay on their feet. Common sense says that if they are on point and have lifted their birds, then as long as they don't run in it doesn't matter whether, on hearing a shot, they sit, stand or lie down. If they are running when a shot is fired over their brace mate it is a different matter and they should certainly acknowledge the shot by dropping or sitting rather than racing on, but if they are already stationary at a point it hardly matters. Even so, I have seen dogs eliminated because they sat rather than dropped flat when a shot was fired or when birds rose from a point.

Indirectly it is negative judging that leads to some judges feeling the need to 'protect' their winning dogs in the later rounds of a trial. If you have already eliminated dogs for minor, technical infractions in the first round then what do you do if your best dog makes a similar minor mistake right at the end of three rounds of first class work?

You can act with complete consistency and eliminate him – and give first prize to a dog that was inferior overall on the day but just didn't happen to make any small mistakes. Or you can decide that all the previous good work overrides a minor error right at the end and give him first prize anyway. But just hang on a moment. Suppose one of the dogs you eliminated for making the same mistake right at the start of his first run had been allowed to continue and had then produced three rounds of superb work? Using the same logic he should now be in the running for top honours – except that he has been denied the chance to show what he can do.

Should you decide to take part in field trials though it is incumbent upon you to accept the judges' decision with good grace, whether you agree with them or not. A field trial is a sporting contest and everyone involved should, and almost invariably does, behave in a sporting manner. If you run in enough trials there will undoubtedly be as many days when lady luck will favour you as days when she seems to be looking the other way. If you especially dislike the manner in which a particular person judges then don't enter when he or she is judging. The judges' names are always on the schedule that accompanies the entry form and you are completely free to decide whether you want your dog subjected to their style of judging.

Fortunately the great majority of judges do not judge pointer and setter trials in a negative manner and will do their best to give every dog that comes under their scrutiny the best possible chance of showing its merit. What is it that they are looking for in a dog and indeed in the dog's handler?

If I were to try and sum up the requirements of a field trial winner in a single word, then that word would be 'class'. There is something about the very best dogs that stands out almost from the moment they are cast off. It isn't any single attribute: it is rather a combination of all the factors that make up good pointer and setter work. A top class dog will quarter his beat fully

The fruits of victory. A delighted Maurice Getty after winning the 2002 Champion Stake.

and methodically, adjusting his scope to match the prevailing conditions of scent. He should work the whole of the beat evenly, not favouring one side over the other, and he should do so with pace and drive. Pointers and setters have been bred to run, not to potter about, and that desire to cover the ground should be evident from the start.

When he finds birds he should point solidly and confidently and hold that point for as long as the birds will sit in front of him. Once he is ordered to lift them he should rode in freely until the birds rise, then he should drop immediately without any instruction from his handler. If his brace mate points he should back the point as soon as he sees it and remain quite steady while the other dog rodes in and raises the birds. Hares, rabbits and sheep should all be ignored however invitingly they may bob along in front of him. He should be responsive to his handler's whistle, though not so reliant on it that the handler is continually blowing it to turn him and direct him about the beat. And if he is a well built dog with a stylish running action and a striking attitude when on point it will do his cause no harm at all.

So much for the dog: now what about the handler? In many ways a field trial is a team event, the team in this case consisting of dog and handler. As a handler you may not be able to win the trial on your dog's behalf but you can certainly lose it for him. A top class handler with an average dog will win more trials than a top class dog with a less than competent handler.

It is a debatable point as to what comprises good handling. If you have the sort of dog who will settle himself down to quartering a good, wide beat and do so without any advice or assistance on your part then I would suggest that the best possible way of handling him is to stick your hands in your pockets and quietly let him get on with it. If he needs to be turned on the whistle in order to show him the boundaries of his beat then, of course, you must do that,

131

Jean Brown with her English Setter and Wilson Young with a Pointer waiting for their turn.

but, unless he simply will not turn unless you bring him round on the whistle, once he has realised where he should turn then stop whistling. The dog will do his work far better if he is allowed to get into a rhythm and then left to get on with it than if you are constantly chirping and waving at him.

That said, it could also be argued that a dog that turns smartly on the whistle and adjusts his quartering readily on being given a hand signal should impress the judges with his obedience and handleability. And so he might. I very much doubt though that judges are at all impressed by those handlers who have their whistles ready in their mouths even before the dogs are cast off and blast away constantly once he starts running. Noisy handling is a major fault and could cost your dog a place, besides which, the majority of dogs, if subjected to an incessant barrage of whistles and shouts, quickly learn to ignore it and get on with doing their own thing. Then, when you really do need to give them a command, the chances are that they will ignore that one too.

Beware of marching on too quickly when your dog is running. An all too common fault at trials is for handlers to press on far too rapidly. This is probably motivated by a desire to see *their* dog take the leading cast and thus be the one of the brace that finds birds. The danger is, particularly on days when the scent is poor, that by rushing ahead they push their dog into taking too big a bite at the end of each cast in order to stay in front of the handler, thus missing or flushing birds that he would have pointed if allowed to take his natural cast.

You are not allowed to touch your dog when he is on point, though you may stand close beside him and encourage him to rode in by a click of your fingers or a quiet voice command. A blast on the drop whistle or a command to 'Hup!' when the birds get up is usually acceptable at Puppy or Novice level, but could downgrade you in an Open stake. It is much better if the dog drops of his own volition but, that said, a quick 'Hup!' would clearly do you less harm than having him run in.

Stickiness on point is a difficult problem to deal with in a trial. There are few things more frustrating than having seen your dog quarter and point to perfection only to have him stand stubbornly fixed with grouse just in front of him. This is one of those problems that are easily overcome when you are out shooting – you can march on ahead of the dog with the guns ready on either side; you can put him on a lead and give him a tug to get him moving; you can even whistle up the picker-up with his spaniel and let his dog flush the birds. Often all it needs is a gentle touch on the dog or for the handler to cross in front of him and break the scent for an instant. But you can't do any of those things in a field trial.

HM The Queen at an International Challenge Match for Pointers held on her Balmoral Estate.

Part of the problem is that grouse in July and early August tend to sit very, very tightly. The dog is right on top of the covey and scent is so strong that he simply can't move in and flush them. There are several tricks of the trade that competitors use to try and fool the judges. One fine handler, now sadly no longer with us, once told me that he made one of his dogs up to Field Trial Champion by pretending to trip up and falling over noisily just as he reached the dog. The commotion caused by his fall was enough to flush the birds. A discreet nudge on a paw by the handler's boot is not unknown, nor is the practice of innocently inserting a leg in front of the dog's nose to try and break the scent. One competitor is even rumoured to carry a little sand in his pocket and toss it at his dog, disguising the movement in an exaggerated arm movement culminating in a finger snap that is ostensibly intended to click the dog on.

I don't want to give the impression that field trials are filled with competitors bending the rules in order to put one over on the judges because the vast majority of handlers are open, straightforward and completely honest as well as being extremely sporting and genuinely appreciative of good dog work no matter whose dog is involved. If you want to have a go at trials you will find them friendly, helpful and genuinely welcoming to fellow enthusiasts. Provided you are willing to listen you will get plenty of help and advice. Trials are great fun for those taking part and well worth a visit even if you just want to watch. They will certainly give you a good idea of just how exciting and effective a good pointer or setter can be at finding game for the gun.

The question posed earlier was whether they are really the best possible test of the working ability of a pointer or setter. The answer is not perhaps as straightforward as it might seem. Initially I have to side with Mr Teasdale-Buckell and many other authorities here and agree that the modern pointer and setter trial format is no judge of stamina. In the few minutes that a dog is able to perform in front of the judges it is certainly possible to judge his pace and style, to get an idea of the standard of his discipline, to assess the quality of his quartering and, hopefully, to see how well he handles birds. There is though, no possible way to make an assessment of the dogs' stamina: and in the shooting field, stamina is at least as important as any other virtue in a pointer or setter.

A fast pace is an integral part of the style in which pointers and setters work. A dog with pace is exciting to watch and, other things being even, will always find more birds than a slower, plodding type of dog because he will cover more ground in any given period of time. The question we have to ask – and the question that a modern field trial cannot answer, except, occasionally, in the negative – is whether he will be able to keep up that pace for a reasonable length of time.

I do not mean that I would expect a pointer or setter to run flat out all day long. I would though expect any reasonably fit dog to be capable of working several spells of at least thirty minutes in the course of a day. If I can take three dogs to the hill: run each one for an hour before lunch and an hour after: then I have a team capable of matching the needs and fitness of most shooting parties. The type of dog that can produce tremendous pace for four or five minutes only before having to stop and rest is little more than a nuisance on a shooting day. At a field trial the same dog could sweep all before him.

So, if we take stamina into account, as we must, I have to agree with many a previous commentator and say that pointer and setter trials are not a reasonable test of all the abilities that a dog should have in order to be considered a first class shooting dog. Having written that though, I would contend that there is no reasonable way that I can envisage of organising trials in such a way that stamina is truly tested unless the number of dogs allowed to compete is severely restricted – and I am not advocating that for reasons already stated.

On balance I believe that pointer and setter trials do provide a valuable service to the breeds and help to maintain the standards of working dogs at a high level. Whether the words 'field

trial champion' in a pedigree really mean that the holder of the honour is a first class working

Colin Organ and Richard MacNicol shake hands as they go forward for their run.

dog is open to question, but there can be no doubt that, in order to gain the award, he must, in the eyes of two judges, have proved himself superior to thirty or forty other trial winning dogs and done so on more than one occasion.

I have occasionally heard the opinion expressed by owners of working dogs that, if they could only be bothered to compete, they have a dog that would wipe the floor with all those fancy field triallers. It is rare indeed for any of them to be willing to put their money where their mouth is, and rarer still for one of them to be proved correct.

Personally, I very much enjoy watching, photographing and occasionally reporting on trials for the shooting press, but I find I have little interest in competing. Somehow, despite being a fiercely competitive player in thirty odd years of football and rugby, I cannot view shooting and dog work in a competitive light. That said, I have the greatest respect for those who do relish the atmosphere of a trial and nothing but admiration for the high standards of training, handling and birddog work that can be seen there.

Pointer and setter trials may not be the perfect format for judging a working dog, but there is no doubt that they have contributed enormously to raising and maintaining the high standard of gundog work that we have enjoyed in Britain over the past hundred and forty years. Long may they continue to do so.

Shooting over dogs is delightful work.

CHAPTER 9
Field Days

Shooting grouse over dogs is delightful work.
Eric Parker, writing in *Shooting by Moor, Field and Shore,*
The Lonsdale Library 1929

Trying to explain exactly what it is that makes shooting over pointers and setters such, to use Mr Parker's apposite phrase, 'delightful work' is not easy. There are too many different aspects of a day on the hill, and that aspect which most appeals to one may be anathema to another, even though both find shooting grouse over dogs to be 'delightful work'.

Take walking. One man may relish the prospect of tramping for miles over rough moorland, feeling the gritty rasp of rock beneath his boots at one moment and the quivering surface of a blanket bog at another. He may welcome the utter exhaustion, the sore feet and the aching thighs as he eases those boots off at the end of the day: feeling that expending so much physical effort somehow justifies and legitimises taking the lives of the grouse that are laid out in the heather beside him. Another man may detest the effort involved but grudgingly accept it as a price he has to pay in order to go shooting in August.

One man may delight in watching the dogs at work: another may care nothing for the grace and style with which they perform but relish only those moments when an arm is raised to signal a point and he can start forward with his gun at the ready and the prospect of a shot in the offing. Some guns find the way that grouse burst from the heather and curve off across the hill an ample challenge to their shooting skills: others dismiss shooting over dogs as too easy: as

Muzzle-loading day.

offering 'nothing but straightforward going-away shots'. (Incidentally, though I have heard this particular argument on many occasions I have never heard it advanced by a gun who had actually shot grouse over pointers and setters. Many a novice gun starts his first day shooting over dogs believing that all the shots he gets will be simple, but most of them have cause to think again by the end of the day.)

Even the most committed birddog enthusiast will probably admit that, as far as shooting over dogs goes, there are days and then there are days. Walking five miles across the hill under a warm August sun, the dark green and purple of the heather stretching away for miles on every hand and golden pollen rising in clouds to coat your boots and cling to your socks may be truly delightful, but you might as easily be tramping along head down in driving rain, boots soaked through, icy water trickling down your neck and birds so wild that the chance of a point, much less a shot, is about as likely as buying the winning ticket in the national lottery.

Difficult ground, patchy scent, wild birds and fickle winds may be a major source of frustration to some handlers while to others they represent a challenge to be faced and a satisfaction all the greater when the dog uses his brain as well as his nose to give you the chance of a brace of grouse in the bag when earlier none had seemed likely. One handler may love to watch his dog puzzling out the trail as he tracks an old cock grouse, twisting and turning through the peat hags, while another may dismiss such work as fit only for spaniels and pick the dog up and re-cast him. It is perhaps worth mentioning that, while the second handler may be acting in the best tradition of purist birddog work, the first handler will shoot a lot more grouse. You may decide for yourself who gets the best of the bargain.

There are so many variables that go to make up a day on the hill or among the stubble and root fields, that it is impossible to write of a 'typical' day. Rather I will try to convey a few impressions of pointer and setter work, the joy and the frustration, the pleasure of good company, the stirring sight of a pointer or setter flowing effortlessly over the ground and then crashing onto point, the adrenalin rush as a covey bursts out of the heather right under your feet, the sound of shots and the smell of burnt powder, the increasing tug of the gamebag on your shoulder as the day wears on and the satisfaction when you finally return to the lodge at the end of the day with weary dogs, tired legs, sunburnt arms and face and maybe a few grouse in the bag to show for your efforts. Delightful work? It is for me. You must judge for yourself.

One of the problems inherent in keeping a kennel of working pointers and setters is that the season is so short. You have three or four, perhaps five or six, dogs in the kennel: you work them hard for two or three weeks in August: and then that's it for the year. For the next forty-nine weeks they will lie around the kennel, eating their rations and getting fat while serving no useful purpose until next August rolls around. Is this a fair picture of the joys of keeping a kennel of birddogs?

It may be, for some owners, but it doesn't have to be so. If you have the time and the inclination coupled with the ground over which to shoot, then you can extend your working season to at least match, if not actually exceed, the amount of time that owners of more conventional gundogs spend working their dogs. Let us start in the spring and look at some of the ways in which you and your pointers and setters can keep busy throughout the year.

If you have a nearby grouse moor and a friendly keeper the early spring months can be a good time to introduce your dog to game. At this time of the year the paired up grouse are living on the parts of the moor where they will nest and raise their young. Paired grouse are very territorial birds and will soon return to their nesting area after being disturbed. If you have a young dog and are looking to get him a few points without working him too hard, then a grouse moor in spring is an excellent place to do it. Where you find a pair of grouse one day is likely to be pretty much where you will find the same pair of grouse the next time you are on the hill, so you can arrange your dog's work load with rather more precision than at other times of the year.

As far as giving the keeper or shoot manager accurate information about the prospects for the shooting season, spring grouse counts are of limited value. While it is interesting to know how many pairs of grouse have survived the winter it is only after those pairs have raised their broods that any real estimate of shootable surpluses can be made. Nevertheless, many keepers like to know what level of stock the moor holds prior to nesting, and a fine March day on the hill is a wonderful antidote to the gloom of winter. It is also an excellent way of getting your dogs ready for the spring field trial circuit if you are planning to compete.

The spring trial circuit starts in March on the grouse moors of Scotland and then moves south to East Anglia in early April. The weather can play a part in the success or otherwise of a trial at any time of the year, but the spring trials are particularly subject to its whims. Look at the contrast between these two trials held in the Perthshire hills above Amulree.

The first, in the year 2000, was a Novice stake held in glorious spring sunshine. The moor where the trial was run is a big, open bowl surrounded by hills and as the day progressed the smoke from heather burning rose into the sky on all sides. A procession of four-wheel-drive vehicles carried judges, keepers, competitors and their dogs from where we had parked our cars out along a gravel road and high onto the hill. Everyone then had a long walk across the moor in order to allow the dogs to run back into the wind. I had somehow managed to get left behind in the car park and had started to walk up the hill road but as luck would have it I managed to hitch a lift in a passing Argocat that was being used to take Mrs Eppie Buist out to watch the trial.

Mrs Buist is the best possible recommendation for the benefits of owning and working pointers and setters. Well into her nineties, she still takes a lively interest in field trials, shooting and anything else to do with birddogs. I was out on the hills in Sutherland with her on her eightieth birthday when she was training a young dog and had brought him for a first scent of grouse. She recalled being on the same hill nearly sixty years previously, working a team of pointers throughout August for a shooting party. A little less mobile now than she was then her understanding and appreciation of dog work is still as sharp as ever.

An unusually marked Pointer.

139

Mrs Eppie Buist at a pointer and setter field trial.

The trial itself didn't really live up to the promise of the day and only two awards were made, but it was reward enough just to be back on the hill on such a glorious day. Two years later, having lost a whole year's trials during the foot and mouth epidemic of 2001, we were back on the hill for the first pointer and setter trial to be held in almost two years. At least, we should have been back on the hill, but as we drove through the Sma' Glen and half a foot of snow it soon became clear that, short of a very sudden thaw, there was unlikely to be much action that day.

We spent a relaxing and entertaining morning in the hotel while the keeper, the judges and the trial secretary went off to inspect the ground, but it was clearly hopeless. South of Perth it was a pleasant March morning, but up in the hills it was an entirely different matter. Overnight snow and a sharp drop in the temperature meant that trialling was impossible and, in common with many others, we had made a wasted journey.

It is unusual (though not unknown) for snow to cause a spring trial to be abandoned in East Anglia, but the weather can play a big part in the success or failure of trials here as well as those in the north. A late spring that holds back the growth of barley and wheat can mean that there is not enough cover for the partridges and pheasants to sit for the dogs, and cold, wet days can push all the birds out of the fields and into the woods and hedgerows. If the weather is good though and there is reasonable cover in the fields the spring trials can be great fun even if the flat fields of Norfolk and Suffolk are a far cry from the grouse moors where most pointer and setter work is done these days.

Spring trial in Perthshire with the smoke from heather burning drifting across the hill in the background.

141

Since all the game on the ground will be at least a year old and probably well used to avoiding the attentions of dogs and humans alike a spring trial can prove difficult for both handlers and judges. Pheasants will run off through the corn rather than sit when they are pointed, and a running pheasant can cover the ground a good deal faster than a man can walk. If your dog is a hundred yards away when he points the pheasant could well be double that distance from the dog by the time handler, judge and gun arrive and send the dog on to flush the bird. Alternatively, some birds will simply take to their wings well before a dog can get within scenting distance. Sorting out 'false points' and 'flushed' game can be difficult if not impossible at times and adjudicating at a spring trial can be a real test even for the most experienced judges.

Once the spring trials are over and the birds are nesting in the fields and on the moors there are severe restrictions on work for the dogs until July. Sitting hens and young chicks are far too vulnerable to disturbance to risk running pointers and setters through their nesting areas. That said, if you have access to fields where grass is cut for silage, then exercising and training your dogs in those fields may actually be beneficial to ground nesting birds if it persuades them to nest elsewhere.

The modern forage harvester, coupled with the early cutting of grass for silage, has probably done more than pesticides, predation and loss of habitat combined to decimate our ground-nesting birds. Sweeping round the fields at high speed, and generally cutting from the outside inwards, forage harvesters crush clutches of eggs and slice up chicks and sitting hens alike. Game birds are not the only species to suffer: lapwings, curlews, oystercatchers, skylarks and many other birds that were once common in our skies are now rated as endangered species. Running your dogs on moorland where birds are nesting can only make matters worse. On the other hand, if the disturbance from your dogs induces the parents to pick a nest site where they will be safe from the blades of the mower you will have done a little bit towards conservation as well as getting in some out of season training with your dog.

As June moves into July the grouse chicks should be getting strong enough on the wing to be ready for grouse counts and summer field trials to start. The two go hand in hand for many owners, with grouse counting being a way of getting their dogs fit for the trials.

There are other ways to get your dogs fit, but none, I would suggest, that are remotely as much fun as grouse counting. Taking the dogs walking or running on roads will certainly help to get them into trim and toughen up their paws but with the speed of the traffic and the general congestion on our roads today road work may be practically impossible unless you live in one of the more remote parts of the country.

I once, and only once, tried taking some of the Pointers out to trot along with me as I rode my bicycle. Balancing on two wheels while attached by ropes to two or three Pointers, each of whom is heading in a different direction, at some speed, is not something I would recommend. The experiment came to a sudden and somewhat painful end: there was no permanent damage but I have never felt moved to try the running dogs beside a bicycle again. Taking them with me when I went running was more successful, though somewhat disheartening. At my regular pace of about eight miles an hour Zenda – who was our fattest and slowest dog at that time – was moving at little more than an extended trot. If I tried sprinting she would just about deign to break into a canter. When I slowed down to a wheezing trot again after about a hundred yards she would look up at me with a slightly puzzled expression as if wondering what had made me pull up so quickly. The only time I ever managed to out-run one of the dogs was when I took our very first Pointer bitch running a few weeks before the start of the shooting season. In those days I was reasonably fit and we went for a ten mile trot around the back lanes near the pub we used to run in Suffolk. Towards the end of the run I noticed that she was starting to lag behind, but we finished up in fine style. Next morning poor Anouska could hardly walk.

The sudden exercise on hard roads had left her with skinned pads and she was gingerly trying to find a way to limp on all four feet at the same time. Nevertheless, the next time I set out for a run she was there, wincing, but ready to go again no matter how much it was going to hurt. Naturally, I didn't take her, and ever since I have been careful to introduce road work gradually. The paws soon healed and she was ready for the start of the season. Sore paws can also occur when dogs are first taken to the hill, particularly if you are tempted to do too much with the dogs before they have had a chance to get fit and hardened up to their work.

One of the great joys of grouse counting is that there is no pressure on you or the dogs. No worries about whether the dog will hold his point until some overweight gun has lumbered noisily across the moor to where you are waiting: no judges watching every move determined to ask you to pick up at the slightest transgression. No competition, no guns complaining because they have to walk up the hill to reach a point, no pickers-up sending their dogs racing in to collect birds while your dog is still working out the covey. There is just you and your dogs, a few thousand acres of moorland and – who knows? – maybe a few grouse.

It isn't necessarily the total number of grouse that you find that is important. Most keepers will have a pretty good idea of how many pairs of adult birds should have nested on the beat. The information that they need and that a grouse count should provide is how well those nesting pairs have done. The important questions are, how many young grouse are there in each brood and how well grown are those youngsters? Barren pairs, coveys of cheepers or adults with only two or three chicks are bad news: coveys with eight or ten young that are well grown and strong on the wing will quickly put a smile on the face of the dourest keeper. Total numbers mean very little until they are related to the numbers expected on a particular moor.

I have been grouse counting on a hill above the Helmsdale river in Sutherland and seen the keeper delighted because we had found nearly a hundred birds in the course of a long day's dog work. A few years later at Wanlockhead in southern Scotland we found two hundred and fifty plus grouse in just a couple of hours and the keeper was considering cancelling all shooting 'because the birds are just not there'.

The difference, of course, was that the Sutherland hill was primarily a deer forest, the grouse were shot over pointers, and a hundred birds promised good sport to come in a few weeks' time. Wanlockhead is a driving moor and a good year would have seen many more birds on the ground that we had covered. In fact we had been seeing well-grown birds in coveys of reasonable numbers, and when shooting started things were not as bad as the keeper had feared. It is always as well to remember that a grouse count is only a guide to numbers and vagaries of the weather can cause some strange results.

A few years ago we had heavy snow at the end of May and many grouse nests were wiped out. Just before the Twelfth we were asked to take the dogs and do a count on a driving moor a few miles north of our home because the keeper feared that the late snow had been absolutely disastrous for his birds.

He had been out himself a fortnight earlier with his Labradors and found only three or four barren pairs on one of his best beats. We went over the same ground with two pointers and an Irish setter and found covey after covey, though in every case there were only four or five chicks in each, and they only appeared to be four or five weeks old. Plainly the hens had lost their first clutches of eggs in the snow, then laid a second, smaller clutch and hatched off these late broods. What was interesting though was that, at the time the keeper went round with his Labradors the dogs had singularly failed to find them. This is not intended in any way to be a criticism of those Labradors because they are among the very best field trial dogs in the country. The birds must have been sitting so tightly and giving off so little scent that they were

143

undetectable even to a team of first class, experienced dogs, though I have no doubt if the Labs had been out with us on the day the pointers and setter were worked they too would have been able to find the grouse.

A couple of years later it was the heat rather than a snow storm that skewed the results of a grouse count. We took the dogs across to the west coast and another driven moor. It was one of those rare summers in the south of Scotland when day after day is baking hot and even the heather moorland was dry and dusty. We worked our dogs over two of the best beats on the moor and only found a couple of coveys where there should have been at least twenty. It was hard work for the dogs and both puzzling and worrying for the keeper who knew that there had been a good stock of birds on the ground during the nesting season. The odd coveys that we did find were well grown and strong on the wing and, if I remember correctly, were made up of ten or a dozen birds in each case, and there was no sign of any barren pairs as might have been expected if some natural disaster had wiped out the young chicks. This particular story had a happy ending because once the rains finally came the birds flocked back to the moor, having presumably moved off during the heat wave in search of water.

Part of the pleasure of a grouse count may lie in the lack of any pressure, but the same thing cannot be said of a field trial. To run your dog under the eyes of the judges, to strict rules and regulations and in front of forty or so other trainers puts the handler under mental pressure of the most severe kind. It ought not to bother the dogs, but there is no doubt that in many cases the mood of the handler is picked up by the dog. This tension can show in different ways. Normally obedient dogs may ignore their handlers, others may race off wildly and take a while to settle down to hunting properly, and the occasional dog may simply take a dislike to the whole atmosphere of the trials and never show his real potential for work. Others love it and perform at their best in front of a crowd. Much the same can be said for some of the handlers.

One of the most enthralling trials I have attended was the Champion Stake held in Scotland in the year 2000. There is a tendency to feel that a Champion Stake ought to be something special with the competitors performing at an extra high level, though there is no reason why this should be so. The dogs running in the Champion Stake are, by and large, exactly the same dogs that have been running in Open and All-aged stakes throughout the summer circuit, possibly with the addition of a few qualified dogs from Ireland whose handlers make the trip specially for the stake. There is always a large gallery for the event and a lot of extra tension, but logically there is no reason why the Champion Stake should be any better than any other. And yet sometimes it is and the millennium stake was one of those occasions.

Obviously, it requires an excellent level of performance from a significant number of the dogs for a stake to be truly outstanding, and this certainly happened. In addition, the judges – Professor Beazley and Wilson Young – kept the day moving along at a good pace and gave the handlers every chance to show their dogs' capabilities.

The way that the judges handle the day can make a great deal of difference to the quality of a stake. The gallery at a trial want to see dogs at work: not stand around while the judges have endless discussions about which dog did what, and why, in the previous brace. If one dog has flushed birds and the other one has chased a hare it seems pointless for the judges to sit in the heather and hold a long conference before pencilling a line through both names, but it sometimes happens and the trial loses all momentum. There were no such problems on this occasion and the maximum possible time was allotted to actually running dogs with discussion between the judges kept to a minimum.

At the start of the morning the wind was very light and variable: tricky conditions for dogs, handlers and judges alike. The first round was run on a wide-open expanse of moorland that looked almost flat from a distance but actually consisted of numerous humps and hollows with

144

Grouse counting on a hot day: leading a young Irish Setter in to a covey of grouse.

Wilson Young and the Reverend Professor John Beazley were the judges for the 2000 Champion Stake.

some quite big areas of tall rushes breaking up the heather. Without a steady breeze to dictate the direction of the beat the judges sensibly indicated a line of march to the handlers and then left them and their dogs to work out the problem in their own ways. It was fascinating to watch the first two or three brace and see how different dogs handled the vagaries of the breeze: some quartering across the beat as if the wind was blowing into their faces, others swinging back and curving round to hunt across the wind even as it was changing.

As the morning progressed the breeze steadied and rose enough to make things easier for the later competitors and the overall standard of work stayed high. There was a brief period towards the end of the round when scent seemed to fail and several dogs were eliminated for flushing birds or missing them altogether despite seeming to have had every chance of pointing them. This brought us to lunch and then the judges called back five brace for a second round.

The standard of work in the morning had been exceptionally good and after the break things got even better. The first brace to run were Penny Darragh with an Irish Setter and Colin Organ handling a Pointer for its owner, Prue Crooke-Hurle. These two produced what was undoubtedly the best work of the day, quartering their ground superbly and demonstrating to the gallery just what it is that makes pointer and setter work, at its best, such an enthralling prospect. The sheer athleticism of the dogs: the intensity of their concentration as they point, the

Colin Organ and Penny Darragh gave a superb display of pointer and setter work to clinch first and second places respectively.

147

hot August sun and some of the finest scenery on the country is more than enough of itself, but when you mix in the very real tension felt by handlers who are just one good run away from winning the most coveted prize in the field trial world the day takes on an almost surreal aspect.

More excellent work followed, though there was nothing quite as good as that first run from Penny and Colin. Four dogs came back for the third and final round: Penny and Colin to run together again and then Richard MacNicol with a Pointer and Colin Organ handling a Pointer for my wife, Georgina. Once again the setter and the Pointer ran superbly for Colin and Penny but this time the Pointer just edged the run when the setter paused and dropped her head to investigate a whiff of scent and the Pointer took the ground ahead of her and produced another covey of grouse. The final brace went through the formality of their run and then it was back to the meet to hear the judges announce the winner: Colin Organ with Prue Crooke-Hurle's Pointer bitch, Field Trial Champion Gerensary Zephyr of Sparkash. Penny Darragh was runner up with her Irish Setter Erinvale Jig with third and fourth places going to Richard MacNicol's Pointer Traighmhor Top Class and Georgina Hudson's Pointer Madrua McKeever, handled by Colin Organ.

The sheer quality of the work coupled with a great day on the hill in excellent company made this probably the best trial I have ever seen or am ever likely to see. Other days at trials have been just as memorable, though not always for the same reasons.

Lord Mansfield presents the winner's trophy to Colin Organ.

FIELD DAYS

Quite a few years ago we were on holiday in Ireland and decided to enter an Irish Setter bitch called Syringa in a trial that was being run locally. The meet was arranged for nine-thirty in the village square. Punctuality not being a dominant feature of life in Donegal, I was more than a little surprised when, on the stroke of nine-thirty, everyone decanted from their vehicles and headed into the nearest hotel. Naturally we joined them. As we crossed the square I checked with the nearest person that we were, as I assumed, going in to the hotel in order to hold the draw for the running order. He looked at me with a mixture of sympathy and surprise.

'We are not,' he said. 'We're going in for a drink.'

Still thinking that the draw would surely take place once the more hardened drinkers had snatched a quick half, Georgie and I sat quietly in a corner of the bar and were pretty much ignored until, realising that the words 'quick' and 'half' were totally at odds with what was actually going on, we decided to join the throng around the bar. Once we each had a glass in our hands we became part of the crowd and after the second, or possibly third, glass nothing seemed more natural than to be drinking whisky at breakfast time as a prelude to a field trial. It certainly calms the nerves.

The draw did take place eventually – at about eleven 'o'clock – and then we all set off in search of the Donegal pheasant. The day was wonderfully disorganised in complete contrast to the strict discipline of an English trial. We travelled around in a convoy of vehicles, running a couple of brace here and three brace there until everyone had had a run. Sometimes there was a pheasant or a snipe, mostly there wasn't, but there was great enthusiasm and some excellent dog work, the craic was good and overall the day was great fun. The only problem was the weather, which was what the Irish call a 'soft day' (i.e. raining more or less heavily, most of the time) but that just meant more time in the bar between showers. It may not be trialling as we know it on this side of the Irish sea, but it has a lot to recommend it once you get over the first shock of washing down your corn flakes with a slug of Bushmills.

However seriously you take your trials and your grouse counts – and some people take trials very seriously indeed – there is nothing to match the feeling that you get as you slip the first dog and set out across the hill on the morning of the Twelfth. There are two hundred and fifty odd years of tradition behind you and a whole season stretching out ahead. In an ideal world the sun would be shining, the grouse would be there, sitting tightly in well grown coveys of ten or more, the dogs would work perfectly and the guns would never miss a shot. In the real world things may be a little different, but whatever the outcome there is always a little extra thrill to being on the hill at the very start of the season. Never mind all the nonsense in the media about the 'crack of high-powered rifles in the glens as rich sportsmen slaughter expensively reared birds'. To set out in the wake of thousands of other pointer and setter enthusiasts, to work your dogs in exactly the way that they have done over the centuries, is to perpetuate a fine sporting tradition: and to hell with political correctness, ignorant politicians, interfering bunny-huggers and all the other idiots that are conspiring to ruin our countryside and our way of life.

Because it *is* the Twelfth the start of the season somehow seems that little bit more important than any other day and calls for an extra polish of the boots, a collar and tie instead of an open necked shirt and, if it isn't raining, the good tweed jacket rather than a Barbour. Our usual meeting place is at the gate at the bottom of the hill road and once everyone has arrived and been introduced we drive up and park by the pumping station at the hydro-electric scheme dam. There is an interminable delay for the dogs as everyone laces their boots, sorts out guns and cartridges, havers over whether to carry a stick or not (always do so: a good stick is essential on the hill), piles packed lunches, coats, leggings and spare cartridges into the Argocat, listens to Jeremy's brief chat about the rules for the day, locks the car, unlocks the car to get something they have forgotten (ear plugs, midge repellent, camera, sunglasses…), locks the car again, wonders where to leave the keys, and then, finally, we are ready to go.

149

Going in to the point while shooting through newly ploughed forestry ground.

Working with pointers and setters can take you into some wild and spectacular country.

Dr Clarke, dressed appropriately for a hot day on the hill, with an English Setter.

If the wind is in the usual quarter our first beat starts with the breeze on our backs as we work across the low ground towards the foot of the ridge. There are never many birds among the little humps and hollows but if we are lucky one of the dogs may find an old cock or even a covey to get the guns into the spirit of things. We head in the general direction of the radio mast and then turn right to start the steep climb up onto the ridge.

Once we reach the top – usually in a straggling line as the less lively members of the party wheeze up the last few feet and wonder why they didn't put more effort into getting fit – we can turn into the wind and the work for the dogs becomes simpler. In a good year this high ground can hold a lot of grouse, and with shorter heather and relatively level walking the going is a lot easier than on the climb up. The ground falls away on either hand though, so a lot of the time the dogs are out of sight and we have to weave from side to side to check whether they are on point or still running. We are quite near the boundary here and every year, without fail, one of the dogs will point a big covey just over the march and we will be forced to watch them glide away without a shot being fired. They never, ever fly onto our ground: always away onto the neighbour's patch. No doubt they would do exactly the same, only the other way round, if our neighbours were the ones out shooting.

A point, when it does happen, can come in any number of ways. It may be in the classic scenario of countless paintings and articles, with the dog standing rigid, front paw raised, head high in the air and the grouse crouching in the heather ten yards in front of his nose as the guns walk in from behind him. On the other hand, all that may be visible could be the tip of a tail as the dog points in the bottom of a peat hag: he may be balanced on the edge of a rock face, twisting his body to get a fix on the scent drifting down from above: he may be laying flat in the heather or crouched down on his elbows or hardly pointing at all but simply standing still and waiting for the guns to come up to him before he goes on to investigate a little a whiff of grouse scent that might mean there is a bird, or a covey, fifty yards ahead. Whatever the circumstance, once a dog is on point a new sense of purpose brings spring to tired legs and a little rush of adrenaline to everyone in the party.

The guns start forward; keyed up in their excitement, unsure whether the point will produce a barren pair, a big covey, or even, perish the thought, a pipit or a lark. The handler is more concerned that the dog will stay steady and the grouse sit tightly until the guns are within range and assured of a shot. The dog himself is probably the most relaxed player in the scene because he knows what it is he's pointing and probably has a pretty good idea whether the birds are sitting tightly or shuffling uneasily and about to take to their wings. Back with the gallery the Cocker spaniel is quivering in anticipation of a retrieve. The time between spotting the dog on point and getting the guns into position can seem interminable but probably isn't more than a couple of minutes, and then, finally, everyone is ready and the handler tells the dog to 'get on'.

Getting the birds on the wing isn't always as simple as it might seem. Yes there are times when the whole operation follows the textbook: the dog rodes in for a couple of yards and the grouse obligingly rise from the heather straight ahead of him, but there are other times when everyone – dog, handler and guns alike – has to work for the birds.

We were crossing a steep-sided gully with a little burn gushing through the bottom and long heather growing on either side. Henry, a pointer, had stopped to lap a few mouthfuls of water as he crossed the burn and then loped off through the long heather and out of sight on the hill above us. The rest of the party paused for a rest by the burn before tackling the slope and the long heather ahead. After a few minutes, when Henry hadn't reappeared, I crossed the burn in his wake and toiled up the hill to see what he was doing.

He wasn't doing anything much at all, being solidly on point a hundred yards or more out on the flat. I went back to where I could see the guns and signal a point and then waited while one gun and Georgina climbed the hill to join me. The others were enjoying their rest and were loathe to move on again so soon. It had been a long day, the sun was hot and we still had a mile or two to cover before we would be back at the dam. Georgina and the gun made their way over to where Henry was still standing motionless on point and she clicked him on to flush the birds. Henry roded in a few yards, turned his head to the left and then back cast; ran twenty yards and pointed again.

Georgina and gun duly adjusted their position: Henry roded in… and then back cast for a second time before pointing again. He roded in, dropped his head and investigated a bit of foot scent and then re-cast yet again. All this was taking quite a bit of time and when Henry pointed for the fourth, or possibly the fifth, time the rest of the shooting party had arrived at the top of the gully and were watching the performance with interest. One final point, and suddenly an old cock grouse exploded out of the heather and was dropped by a single shot from a delighted gun.

Now, there is nothing whatsoever to complain about when the dog points and the birds rise bang in front of him as soon as he rodes in, but for teamwork between dog, handler and gun, not to mention real intelligence on the part of the dog, there is nothing to beat trying to outwit an old grouse, running and twisting through the heather and doing his best to get out of range before he takes to his wings. Determination from the dog and confidence on the part of the gun that, if he persists he will be rewarded by a shot, is only part of it. The dog has to take great care not to crowd the grouse into rising while the gun is out of range, and it helps a lot if the gun is able to read the situation and get himself into the right position without delay or the need

Breaking for lunch among the rocks and heather of the moors above Balmoral.

for lots of instructions from the handler. It also helps if he can shoot straight, especially after all that hard work from the dog.

As the grouse season draws on into September and October, so the grouse themselves become ever more wary. The purple heather phase only lasts a few weeks at best and by the beginning of autumn the hill will be transformed as the deer grass turns brown, berries glow reddish-orange on the rowan trees and the first stags start to roar with the onset of the rut. There may still be a good stock of birds on the hill but making a decent bag is far harder. When we lived in Sutherland we sometimes used to take the dogs out after grouse right through to the end of the season in December. I have a picture on the wall in front of me as I write showing a pointer at work above Loch Choire. The heather under his feet is sere and brown, the loch is a cold, grey with white-capped waves whipped up by a December gale and in the background there is snow lying on the sides of Ben Klibreck, yet as I remember that day the grouse were still sitting well enough for us to enjoy some shooting. Further south though, the birds are often far too wild for dogging long before the end of October and the start of winter proper. I don't know whether this is something to do with the grouse, the type of hill they live on, or pressure of shooting earlier in the season, but it certainly seems to me that the further north you go the later in the year it stays possible to shoot grouse over pointers and setters.

153

I know, from reading old books and articles, that this idea of grouse sitting tighter at the end of the season in the north than they will further south is not original. Grouse certainly are wilder on wet and windy days than they are when there is sunshine and a light breeze, but if anything this would suggest that the further north you go the wilder they should be, when my own observations suggest the opposite. The 'rule' certainly isn't set in stone, and there have been days in Perthshire when the birds have sat well even in late October. There was also one memorable August day in Sutherland when they were as wild as if it had been the end of the season.

It was actually the Twelfth and I see from my diary that the day was misty and cool with a south-easterly breeze. We were working a Pointer called Charlie and a German Shorthaired Pointer with the German being responsible for the retrieving. My comments, written that evening were: 'Strange scenting day. Long carry on scent, dogs winding birds from well back – sixty to seventy yards – but having problems producing them when in close. Both dogs had several non-productive points, quite convinced that there were birds but not being able to produce them.'

The birds behaved that day as if we were well into the season and they had been shot over several times already, showing a wariness of the dogs that doesn't usually manifest until weeks or months later in the year. I remember phoning a couple of the keepers from down the strath that evening and finding that they had experienced much the same problems, with scent being

Even a wet day can't spoil the fun for this Gordon Setter.

Two Irish Setters tethered to a walking stick while the shooting party break for lunch.

difficult and the birds acting wild. Three days later, shooting over Charlie again and his litter sister, Clancy, the same guns who had been out on the Twelfth shot seventeen and a half brace and broke the estate record. There was no problem with patchy scent or wild birds that day. The German pointer had been left in his kennel having injured his shoulder and Charlie retrieved all the birds, much to his delight, and mine.

My employer at Loch Choire, the late Lord Joicey, relished the challenge of shooting grouse over dogs in October and November, when their very wildness made the sport so much more challenging than when they were sitting tightly in the August heather. His German Pointer bitch, Tiger, was a real expert at hunting down grouse as they ran through the peat hags, working on both foot scent and air scent as she puzzled out their trail with Lord Joicey striding along beside her, gun at the ready. Shooting October grouse is almost like stalking, trying to use the contours of the ground to get as close to the point as possible without letting the birds spot your approach, then staying with the dog as he works out the point on birds that may have run well away from the find while he was waiting for you to reach him.

Sometimes late season grouse can be almost impossible to shoot over dogs in the conventional way. We were once invited to take a couple of dogs to a moor near Leadhills at the end of November so that the owner and a few friends could try to shoot grouse over pointers. The wind was blowing half a gale and the grouse were as wild as I have ever seen them, so there was virtually no chance of them sitting to the dogs. Even so the guns managed to make a bit of a bag. The dogs – we were working a Pointer and an Irish Setter – were finding and pointing grouse with no difficulty despite the gale, but the birds were up and away long before any of us could get near the point. The wind was so strong that they were forced to fly back over where the guns were following along behind the dogs and by the time they reached us, with the wind under their tails, they were going like smoke. That the guns managed to hit any was a bit of a surprise, but thanks to some truly spectacular shooting we ended up with three brace in just over an hour on the hill. It wasn't really 'shooting over dogs' but it was great fun for everyone – except for the grouse.

I don't know how many people shoot partridges over pointers and setters nowadays but I suspect that the number will be very low. The days when there were stubble fields left after harvest with enough cover to shelter partridges when they were pointed have long gone and though an increasing number of shoots release partridges every year they are shot in drives rather than over dogs.

A few years ago I tried to establish a hill partridge shoot with the intention of using the birds to train the dogs and then shooting a few over the pointers and setters later in the year. The partridges were trickle released from several small pens in 'coveys' of about twenty-five birds and soon established themselves on the hill. The major problem, as far as shooting them over dogs was concerned, was that they tended to establish themselves with territories very close to the original release sites. Once you know where to find your birds there isn't any real need for a pointer or setter to 'find' them for you. There was also another snag in that the birds soon became far too wary to sit for a dog.

We had a lot of fun trying to shoot over the dogs during the first season and as there were snipe, a few grouse and the occasional woodcock on the hill as well as our partridges the dogs did manage to do some useful work. We even shot a few birds over the dogs. I can still see Perry, a big Irish Setter dog, pointing a covey in the heather above a steep-sided gully. My shooting partner and I each took one bird as they burst into the air and wheeled away down the gully. Mostly though they would be up and off before we could get into range. After that first season we found that the hill partridges worked better as a driven shoot and tended to use the pointers only for an occasional walk round to see if we could find any grouse or snipe with a point on partridge being a bonus.

The essence of pointer and setter work is using the dogs to find game that would be difficult to find by any other means. When we were living in Sutherland our home was at the head of a loch in a glen between two mountains. A strip of mainly birch woodland ran along the sides of the loch and between October and December acted as a staging post for woodcock on their migration flight. The woods were quite steep and rocky with little burns cutting through them and tumbling down to the loch. There were never very many woodcock: half a dozen found while working the dogs along the three and a half miles of the loch side would be rated as a good day: but those that were there tended to sit quite tightly. The chances of stumbling across one while just walking through the woods were minimal, but some of the pointers became experts at finding them during the short winter days.

It wasn't easy work for the dogs because the trees, tumbled boulders and broken ground meant that they could never get any real rhythm into their running. It was all stop and go, twisting and turning through the trees, jumping across burns and picking their way carefully over tangle heaps of fallen rock. The more flashy runners never mastered the work and would wear themselves out trying to gallop at top speed, but the steadier dogs soon learned to pace themselves. I don't recall that we ever shot many birds, but working through those woods on a frosty day with the light fading, a few flakes of snow in the air and a woodcock flickering away through the birches is as good a way of spending a cold winter afternoon as you will find

Armed with a muzzle-loader, this gun seems to confirm that shooting over dogs is, indeed, delightful work.

anywhere. It is also one of the more challenging ways of shooting over dogs as the woodcock jink and twist between the trees and vanish completely unless you are very quick and very accurate with the gun.

One Pointer bitch in particular was a real woodcock expert. She would set out with Georgina along the loch side path to our chicken run, sidle away up the hill and suddenly come on to point in a bracken patch. If we had a stalking party in residence Georgie would leave her there and go back to the lodge, find one of the sportsmen, wait while he grabbed a gun and a couple of cartridges then lead him back to where Clancy would be waiting patiently, still pointing 'her' woodcock. On one memorable occasion the gun shot the woodcock and Clancy went to retrieve it. On her way back, with the first woodcock still in her mouth, she pointed a second one. Sadly, the gun was so surprised that she could scent a live woodcock despite having her mouth full of dead woodcock that he missed it cleanly.

There isn't usually much call for pointers and setters on low ground, driven shoots. Too much game, lots of other dogs milling about and stealing their points, plus the very real problem of seeing them at all if they come on to point in thick cover means that generally the best place for a birddog on a driven day is lying at home in the kennel. There can be exceptions to the

157

rule of course, and I have sometimes used one of the old dogs in the beating line when I didn't have a spaniel or Labrador available. After he became too old to go to the hill, Charlie, one of the best Pointers I ever worked, loved pottering about on a little syndicate shoot where I used to go beating and never seemed to be too bothered if one of the other dogs nipped in and flushed the bird he was pointing. I wouldn't recommend taking a young dog out beating though, unless you are quite certain that you won't be using him again in his proper role as a pointing dog at some time in the future.

Once the pheasant and partridge shooting comes to a close at the beginning of February there are only a few weeks to wait before the first of the spring trials and the start of a new season. Most of us are not fortunate enough to have the leisure time coupled with sufficient finances to allow us to attend spring, summer and autumn trials, go grouse counting pre-season, work our dogs on the hill for the grouse, come down to the low ground for partridges, fit in a few days after snipe and woodcock and perhaps even pheasants and still meet the demands of work and family, so we have to pick and choose our pleasures. More days shooting will mean less time spent at the trials: grouse shooting in August may have to be sacrificed to allow more time at the partridges in September. Few of us can spend as much time as we would like working our dogs, and perhaps that is part of the reason why we take so much pleasure in the time we can spend with them. If there were no constraints then perhaps, just perhaps, the thrill of working pointers and setters might begin to pall.

But as long as I wish for more time to spend with my dogs: more time to attend the trials, more time to go shooting, more time for training and grouse counting and simply enjoying their company, then I think I can agree wholeheartedly with Eric Parker, whose words opened this chapter. Shooting over dogs, or trialling them, training them and working them for others to shoot is, truly, delightful work.

I hope that I will be able to delight in it for many years to come.

INDEX

(Numbers in italics refer to illustrations)